PARISH
BACK
TALK

PARISH
BACK
TALK

The Lyman Beecher Lectures, 1963

BROWNE BARR

ABINGDON PRESS   New York • Nashville

PARISH BACK TALK

Copyright © 1964 by Abingdon Press

Library of Congress Catalog Card Number: 64-16145

SET UP, PRINTED, AND BOUND BY THE
PARTHENON PRESS, AT NASHVILLE,
TENNESSEE, UNITED STATES OF AMERICA

For the beloved and patient people

of the South Church, Middletown,
Connecticut; the former Second Congre-
gational Church, Waterbury, Connecti-
cut; and the First Congregational
Church, *United Church of Christ,*
Berkeley, California

"I thank my God in all my remembrance of you, . . .
making my prayer with joy,
thankful for your partnership in the gospel
from the first day until now."

—Phil. 1:3-5

CONTENTS

INTRODUCTION

A PROVINCIAL REPORT

The objective faith, what does that mean? It means a sum of doctrinal propositions. . . . The objective faith—it is as if Christianity also had been promulgated as a little system, if not quite so good as the Hegelian; it is as if Christ—aye, I speak without offense—it is as if Christ were a professor, and as if the Apostles had formed a little scientific society.[1]   —Søren Kierkegaard

If this introductory quotation brings offense to some professor or other habitué of the academic world, ecclesiastical or secular, it should be noted at once that the pages of this slender volume are primarily addressed

---

[1] *Concluding Unscientific Postscript,* tr. David F. Swenson (Princeton, N. J.: Princeton University Press, 1941), p. 193.

to those Protestants in and out of schools and seminaries who believe that clergymen study theology in order to have something to preach and that the life of the parish church is determined by the theology it teaches. I propose that this is a seriously mistaken point of view, "as if Christ were a professor," and I hope to encourage you to see its inadequacy and peril.

However, that enterprise sounds very abstract and academic and dull. So before we lose some good, faithful, "untheological" layman, let me assure him that these pages also are designed to encourage those who are not yet quite willing to give up the ordinary parish church as obsolete. So it is that much of the book, especially chapters two and three, presents a report of some of the ways a particular parish church has tried to fill conventional forms with vitality, to bear contemporary and relevant witness to Jesus Christ through the much maligned local American church.

By way of further explanation, it should be said that for seven years I was on the faculty of the Divinity School at Yale University, giving and receiving instruction in such courses as "Fundamentals of Preaching" and "Church Administration." There were less formal occasions for instruction, too, such as an informal and irregular faculty luncheon club and academic committee assignments from "admissions" to "curriculum." At last I felt I had learned enough from my colleagues and my students to return to the front ranks of the church. It was then I accepted a call to the ministry of the First Congregational Church in Berkeley, California. After two or three years in that outpost, my former colleagues thought it would be great fun to call me back to make a report. So they conspired to invite me to deliver the Lyman Beecher Lectures on Preaching in 1963. In 1961 and 1962 these lectures had been delivered by parish ministers who had become professors: Gene E. Bartlett, President, Colgate Rochester Divinity School, and Samuel H. Miller, Dean, Harvard Divinity School. Now the committee had invited a professor who had become a parish minister. Also, they assured me that for 1963, three lectures, instead of the usual five or six in the Beecher series, would suffice. I have never been quite certain how to interpret that provision in the invitation! This volume contains the substance of those three lectures. Some parts of them were subsequently delivered at the Aha Paeaina in Honolulu, Hawaii, in June, 1963, and at Eden Theological Seminary, Webster Groves, Missouri, in the Spring of 1964. The hospitality extended to me in these places far exceeded the usual social amenities, and I here record my appreciation to the faculty and students at New Haven and Webster Groves, and to Joseph J. Bevilacqua of the Hawaiian Evangelical Association and the ministers of the Islands. I am also grateful to my sister, Irene, who provided a quiet place in the Arizona winter for the final preparation of these pages, to my secretary, Mary E. Campbell, who exorcized many an infelicity from them, and to my wife who helps in the putting away of childish things.

The original title, "A Provincial and Parochial Report," was appropriate for the circumstances of the public lectures. Indeed, it could still be employed, inasmuch as this present volume is presented to the reader as a report. It is a report to theological students and seminary professors and other ministers and church officers, and everyone else concerned with the Protestant churches in the twentieth century. The word "provincial" fits for several reasons. For one, it suggests countrified manners and imperfect, unfinished speech. This is not because the report comes from Berkeley, California, in the untamed West, where we use Nobel prizes to stop up the chinks in our log cabins, but because the provincial manner, imperfect and unpolished, may be the only suitable manner for all of us whose prophecy will pass away, whose tongues will cease, and whose knowledge, partial as it is, awaits against the day when we shall understand fully even as we are now fully understood.

However, the phrase "A Provincial Report" was not proposed as an affectation of humility—the parish hound barking at the theological princes—nor is it a feeble effort to rebuke with ill-concealed sarcasm those who hold that New Haven, the home of the Beecher Lectures and other academic enterprises, is a sort of theological London and everywhere else in the kingdom is a rustic backwash. Actually, the title has a bit of boastfulness about it. It was Paul, you remember, who returned from the provinces to report. Although I do not presume that comparison, it is more in the spirit of the apostle than in the spirit of Uriah Heep that this report is made. When "the school" arranges for a missionary or a parish minister to be heard, it is recognizing the necessity for dialogue between "the school" and the church. Let us hope, however, that it may be remembering something of even deeper consequence; namely, that it was the experiences in the provinces of the empire which provided the grist for the earliest Christian theological mill. Without that grist the school may find itself, perhaps has already found itself, simply milling *itself*, which, despite the confusion of the figures of speech, suggests self-mutilation. "As if Christ were a professor, and as if the Apostles had formed a little scientific society."

This "provincial" report seeks to justify itself, not on any marginal grounds nor by squeezing every possible nuance of meaning out of a single word, but on the basic contention and supposition that it is not the theological enterprise, i.e., "the school," which is creative of Christian experience and of church, but that it is Christian experience and church which are creative of theology. In the preface to a volume of Karl Barth's sermons, John Marsh poses the question, "How does Barth's theology preach?" and replies that the question would be better put: "What sort of preaching lies behind this kind of theology?" [2] Yet so far are we removed from that truth that we wonder if we have heard the question correctly, or perhaps the man jests. "What sort of preaching lies behind this kind of theology?" My

[2] Karl Barth, *Deliverance to the Captives* (New York: Harper & Row, 1961), p. 8.

13

word! The order is backwards, we think; it is theology which lies behind preaching! Do we not buy and read books and enroll in classes in order to have something to preach? That is, do we not become professors, do the work of professors, study theology, in order to have something to preach? Is that not the proper order? Is it not theology which lies behind preaching?

Not so. The proper order is immediately clear in the New Testament. Consider the experience of Peter, who is put forth by the writer of Matthew as the representative disciple. He is spokesman for all the disciples, and we may assume that we see and hear more than one man when we see and hear Peter. Certainly with him, his experience of the risen Lord came first! Some New Testament scholars doubly emphasize this fact with the exciting proposal that Peter's confession was part of an Easter story projected back into the life of Jesus. So Rudolf Bultmann.[3] And Oscar Cullmann advocates "the quite possible hypothesis that the original conclusion of Mark's Gospel was lost, and with it the story" [4] of Peter's first meeting with the risen Lord, which is now reflected in the story (Luke 5) of their encounter at the lakeside which resulted in the enormous shoal of fish. In any event, there was first the experience and the proclamation of it and then the theology which explained that proclamation, that preaching. But see

[3] Rudolf Bultmann, *History of the Synoptic Tradition* (New York: Harper & Row, 1963), pp. 257 ff.

[4] Günther Bornkamm, *Jesus of Nazareth* (New York: Harper & Row, 1960).

how we reverse the order: first get the theology, then preach it, then meet the Lord. Is this profound distortion of the proper order, this reversal of the normal sequence, symptomatic of disease in the contemporary church, the disease which grows in the absence of the Holy Spirit? We have the objective faith, its formulation, and the study of its theological abstractions elevated, but the community of faith circumvented and its experience unvoiced and unheard. And so we have, as well, the spectacle of the Christian theologian in pulpit and podium, in cloister and classroom and editorial column, who does not know Christ, and who has hidden or forgotten the embarrassment of his poverty in much knowledge.

"Early in his career Kierkegaard concluded that his entire age had been misled by the increase of knowledge," or so Paul Holmer tells us in his introduction to an edition of *Edifying Discourses.* Kierkegaard

viewed this situation as at once tragic and comic. It was tragic because it meant that people had really forgotten what it means to exist. Personal living was made to appear as an addendum, a mere consequent to objective reflection about the world and things in it. It was comic because it meant that an extraordinary and utterly exaggerated significance had been given to knowledge and, by accident, to the professors. Kierkegaard said that it was so bad that even the clergy were rated on a scale which gave them greater eminence the closer they got to being professors of theology. The upshot of such attitudes was that even religion was made a matter of objective faith.

"The objective faith, what does that mean? It means a sum of doctrinal propositions. . . . The objective faith—it is as if Christianity also had been promulgated as a little system, if not quite so good as the Hegelian; it is as if Christ—aye, I speak without offense—it is as if Christ were a professor, and as if the Apostles had formed a little scientific society." [5]

If we are to be spared both the tragic and comic—or the deadly part of both—in our own exaggerations, in our own little apostolic scientific societies, then we need recognize afresh that the life of the church precedes theology. Then it may be that theology may be creative in its own sphere, in its own crucial function of describing, clarifying, and protecting the church. The provincial church pleads for that assistance, and this report comes to provide some data from the parish for everyone who is concerned with the renewal of Protestantism to consider. Christian theology cannot do its work without the raw material. A bit of that is presented herein. This presentation is made, not to rebuke the theologian in us or the theologian among us, but because the proper work of theology is indispensable, and the grist for its mill must come from the provinces far and near. The outward and formal theological enterprise is carried on by the seminaries of the church, but it is an activity carried on as well by every believer who reflects on the

[5] From Paul Holmer's introduction to: Søren Kierkegaard, *Edifying Discourses* (Torchbook ed. New York: Harper & Row, 1958). Quotation from Kierkegaard, *Concluding Unscientific Postscript*, p. 193.

nature of his faith. The work of theology in the class-room and study is the special professional task of the seminary and of the parish minister. It is a work which includes the function of describing, clarifying, correcting the church and its ministry, but it does not create it. The minister's profession is not less than this, and it must be noted that the task of the theological school is not more, despite contrary pretensions and contemporary dilutions. The theological school does not exist to convert, psychoanalyze, or socialize its own members, but to educate them in the work of theology, and to offer the church the benefit of that discipline.

Günther Bornkamm makes clear the crucial role of theology when he writes in his recent life of Jesus that

the confession of the early Church is heard in many varied forms at baptism and the Lord's Supper, in preaching and teaching. . . . The language in which it is heard changes. It is the language of a particular time and situation, one language, where the gospel is preached before Jews, another where it had to come to grips with mystery religions, with gnostic ideas of redemption, with the cultured religiosity of the Stoics and with the emperor-cult. The Christian faith, one might say, takes possession of heathen ideas and "baptises" them, but heathen things very often change the face of Christianity. Thus, from the first, theology is summoned to the field, and the struggle within Christianity itself begins, a struggle for truth, which yet many a time cannot defend itself from what is false.[6]

[6] Bornkamm, *op. cit.,* pp. 189-90.

And so we summon theology again to its proper role, freed of its comic and tragic distortions, for the struggle within Christianity continues and the difficulty of the church in defending itself from what is false has not been buried with Paul or Luther. That difficulty is especially sharp in the provinces, out in the local parish church in America, where the devil delights to confuse and confound the issues with words like "budget" and "practical" and "scientific." Although we no longer speak, as Bornkamm does, of "heathen things" changing "the face of Christianity," we, too, have a language of our particular time and place. We say, rather, that the church has accommodated itself to culture, or we lament the infection of the church by the ideology of the business community and its chief hawkers or by the presumptions of science. The terminology changes for the encounter with the Jews, the gnostics, and the Stoics, with the psychologizers, the positivists, and the commercializers; but the struggle is the same, this struggle within Christianity itself, "a struggle for truth," a struggle to defend itself from what is false. This volume is offered in the hope that its few ounces may be felt in that defense.

The circumstances of this book deserve further clarification, or else I will be guilty of taking credit for what is not mine to take. Most ministers I know, who are professionally content, claim that they did not become ministers, so far as they know, because someone exhorted them to do so, but because somewhere along the line they knew a minister to whom they responded affirmatively. I am indebted to Vere V. Loper for being the sort of minister a mixed-up high-school lad could admire and approach thirty years ago. I am even more indebted to him for a ministry of twenty-one years in Berkeley, of such integrity that insofar as this book tells the story of that parish it is not his story or my story nor the story of our excellent colleagues through the years and now, but the story of all the people and all the ministers and all the secretaries and singers and sextons of a warm and wonderful parish.

C. A. Anderson Scott reported the experience of an officer of one of the Allied Armies in the First World War, indifferent to religion, who strayed into a London church and left the service a humble believer.

According to his own account, it was not anything in the matter of the sermon which produced the change. What he was impressed and moved by was something in the manner of the preaching and whole conduct of the service; but far more, it was something in the demeanour of the people throughout the service, their reverence and obvious concentration on things of supreme moment, which produced in him an overwhelming sense of the reality of the worship which was being offered and of the truth of the Gospel by which it was inspired.[7]

Many strangers have discovered such transforming "demeanour" among the people of our parish, not alone in

---

[7] C. A. Anderson Scott, *The Church, Its Worship and Sacraments* (London: SCM Press, 1927), p. 44.

public worship in our chaste New England meeting-house, almost within sight of the Pacific Ocean, but as our people move out into the world as the church. Most of this book is their book, and the reader will understand the confidence I have in them and in their charity when he sees that I have dared to put these lectures in print. It was one thing to say some of these things three thousand miles from home, but it is quite another to give them the publicity and finality of the printed page. To this patient and provocative flock I am grateful beyond measure, a gratitude which is shared by all the ministers of our parish, past and present.

If half of this book can be blamed on the good and patient people of the Berkeley church, the other half can be blamed on my former colleagues at Yale Divinity School. Their invitation inspired it, but, more importantly, their godly and ungodly conversation through the years has largely shaped the point of view herein expressed. When I first began to prepare the lectures, I wrote to one of them to help me find a technical essay I had once read in a highly specialized professional journal with which I presumed he would be acquainted. His reply helped establish my determination simply to make a report on parish life out in the provinces. He wrote:

I'll give you my first reactions to your remarks on the Beecher Lectures. . . . My first reaction was "here is a Beecher Lecturer going wrong. We ask a man for what he himself is and for the particular insights and wisdom he himself can communicate; so he starts making a frantic search through the scholarly literature for fugitive articles. The end of this course can only be catastrophe. . . ." I imagine that if we want a lecture on the relationship of group therapy to a doctrine of the church, we can probably get a better one from someone else. Now, if you still want me to try to track down the article . . . I will.

My former colleagues were running true to form, and I decided that it would be best if *I* did.

So this report is placed in your hand, with the hope that somewhere out in the provinces some pastor and people, who have been pommeled by the sociologists and intimidated by the professors, will read and take heart again.

I
TROUBLES IN THE PARISH

A Christian was asked if the gospel were being preached by his new minister. He replied that he was sure it was because every Sunday fewer and fewer people came to hear it. This old story must be the proof-text of many critics of the contemporary church, for in a day of tremendous increase in church membership and church attendance, there is also a tremendous surge of despair over the conventional church in America.

This despair does not arise simply from an automatic and cynical distrust of institutional prosperity itself. It rests on impressive evidence in the whole fabric of Western society that the Protestant witness is muted where relevant, and irrelevant where loud. Evidence of trouble in the parish church is found out in the world where the church is meant to be. That world is a world of commerce and of science and of government. Is the church there? Do the leaders of that world demonstrate any dependence on the Protestant witness? Indeed, do they even demonstrate awareness of their substantial past indebtedness to it?

Inasmuch as many members of our society, including not a few middle-class Protestants, drive Fords and Thunderbirds and twist General Electric disposals three times a day and watch anxiously the rise and fall of United States Steel stock, it occurred to me that a book prepared with the financial assistance of the Foundations of these three vast economic enterprises would be of interest. A new course in the Graduate School of Business at Columbia University was recently launched and a textbook was prepared for it with the assistance of grants from these foundations. The course was proposed as "a study of the major ideas and institutions that make up an important part of the environment within which business transactions take place. The ideas would be those philosophical concepts which have helped shape business and society and which continue to compete for the people's loyalty." [1]

---

[1] Richard Eells and Clarence Walton, *Conceptual Foundations of Business* (Homewood, Ill.: Richard D. Irwin, Inc., 1961), from the Preface.

There are 514 pages in the body of the book. On page 490 the final chapter begins. It is entitled "Business and Value—Forming Institutions." Three institutions, the church, the school, and the state, are then presented as such institutions. *Eight* pages are devoted to the church, including all brands of Christianity as well as Islam and Judaism! The substance of the section on the church is that "there is need for theologians themselves to bring to ritual and symbol a greater relevance for modern social needs, to effect a more satisfying reconciliation between faith and reason." That comprehensive judgment on the church is followed by an impressive indictment of business which needs to admit "that in a complex industrial society their special functions are heavily tinged with a *teleology* closely allied to *theology;* consequently, *professional competence may require some immersion in theological waters.*" [2] (Italics mine.) The evidence that these few pages bring to support the thesis of trouble in the parish church is symbolized by the fact that all the erudition of the Graduate School of Business at Columbia and all the resources of these three well-endowed foundations could not conspire to spell "Calvinism" correctly or to discover the correct title of the National Council of Churches.

I cite this experience not to criticize the Columbian scholars, but to underline the deepest kind of trouble in Protestantism: an apparent irrelevance. Tacked on at the end of a book, which presumes to examine the con-

[2] *Ibid.,* p. 498.

ceptual foundations of business with thoroughness and scholarly objectivity, is a superficial and uncorrected essay dealing in a few paragraphs with the religion which many competent observers believe set the stage for the rise of capitalism. In an important treatise described as "An Outline of the Major Ideas Sustaining Business Enterprise in the Western World," [3] the ecclesiastical descendants of Calvin and Luther are treated as an addendum! This testimony to trouble in the parish church can be matched only by the amazement of contemporary Protestant businessmen that there is *any* relation whatsoever between business and religion, other than a few superimposed moral axioms such as "Thou shalt not steal."

This illustration from the commercial world could be matched a thousandfold in the world of science. Competent scholars point out that modern science became possible only in a culture dominated by Christian presuppositions in regard to the nature of creation. And certainly scientific advance has been opened up by that famous and unruly and too frequently disinherited child of Protestantism, education. "Whatever may be the nature of the connection between Christian theology and the origins of modern science," writes Alan Richardson, "it can hardly be without significance that the scientific attitude arose in a civilization which acknowledged one God, who was personal, rational and dependable, and that the most ardent and dedicated

[3] This is the subtitle of Eells and Walton, *op. cit.*

pioneers of the new scientific movement were themselves devoted students of the Bible and of Christian theology." [4] Yet despite this profound interdependent relationship between Christian theology and modern science, it is alarming to discover how many otherwise well-educated and intellectually sophisticated persons believe that the only relationship between the two is expressed by the polite curtsy each one makes to the other upon public occasions, acknowledging the legitimate but separate world the other occupies.

These illustrations from the world of commerce and the world of science could be matched as well by evidence of the widespread ignorance of relationship between Protestant thought and constitutional democracy. It is scarcely ever noted that a government of "checks and balances" was the natural and inevitable consequence of the reasoning of a people who believed in the biblical doctrine that all men were created equal. For this equality was an equality of corruption, and, therefore, no man was qualified to rule absolutely over any other man. If the law and government under which we live rest in large measure upon such biblical doctrines of man's creaturehood and responsibility, then the absurdity of slogans about not mixing religion and

[4] Alan Richardson, *The Bible in the Age of Science* (London: SCM Press, 1961), by permission. *See also:* R. G. Collingwood, *An Essay on Metaphysics* (London: Oxford University Press, 1940), chap. 1.

A. N. Whitehead, *Science and the Modern World* (Pelican ed. Baltimore: Penguin Books, 1938).

Langdon Gilkey, *Maker of Heaven and Earth* (Garden City, N. Y.: Doubleday & Co., 1959), chap. 5.

politics becomes clear. What also grows clear is the irrelevance of the contemporary church in this area, an irrelevance often aggravated by churchmen who seek to remedy the situation by identifying, in an absolute fashion, God's will with some particular and partisan measure. Here the profound implications of the doctrine of original sin are not ignored by the world, but by the church itself.

This kind of evidence bespeaks deep and tragic trouble in American Protestantism—far deeper trouble than can be cured by the rising ecumenism or a new church-school curriculum. Outwardly, this trouble is symbolized by the cathedrals of our century—the Empire State Building and the suburban high school—both dominating their surroundings and competing as the locus of allegiance for modern man. The New England meetinghouse, like the medieval cathedral, is a curious and beautiful anachronism, viewed by tourists on the same day they visit Old Ironsides or have their pictures taken playfully in the stocks.

Every man views these troubles and their sources differently, and would report on them with varied emphases and understanding. The reporter's own bias and vested interest and blind spots, his education and training and experience, his frustrations and idiosyncrasies, influence his report. I write here as a pastor of a conventional Protestant church in twentieth-century America. I may reveal a chip on my shoulder which grows larger with each offhand dismissal of the conventional church as an outmoded institution quite beyond renewal. I simply do not believe that is true. However, as a concerned Christian I am not unaware of the trouble besetting Protestantism in America, and as a parish minister I am convinced that those troubles must be faced and grappled with in the parish church. Furthermore, I do not believe they can be handled by organizational manipulation or improved methods of public relations. I believe that every evidence which is presented of the weakness and irrelevance of American Protestantism is symptomatic of long-standing trouble in the local parish, and that this trouble is in every instance fundamentally theological in nature. That is, it reflects indifference to or misunderstanding of the peculiar religious testimony of the main stream of Protestant Christianity.

In citing the widely presumed irrelevance of Protestant life and thought in the worlds of commerce and science and government, I have endeavored to sketch some outward symptoms of the deep troubles which afflict contemporary Protestantism. Many other outward symptoms of the same troubles could be produced from the worlds of art and education and social service. There is no shortage of symptoms, but what is the source of the trouble? Insofar as that trouble is manifested in or arises from weakened Protestantism, we find again and again, when tracking it down, one or another serious theological corruption or distortion in the life and work of the local parish. I wish to have you consider three such distortions which afflict the life of the ordinary liberal-minded Protestant parish out in the cities and suburbs, towns and countrysides of our land. As we seek to describe these three centers and sources of trouble, will you try to think of the church, not in its grand conclaves in distant places or as a subject of historical inquiry, but in terms of some specific community of persons you know who still assemble for public worship each Sunday? That effort may be difficult or depressing, but it will add a measure of reality to our considerations. If this chapter becomes too theoretical for your Ben Franklin mind, come back to it after reading the other two.

I

First of all, the life of the church is impoverished and emaciated by the pervasive assumption that the church, most certainly in its local manifestations, is man's creation, not God's. Of course, the church is a human institution, and we are helped to a more realistic understanding of it by interpretation which employs principles from the social sciences and social philosophy, as James M. Gustafson has so ably done in his recent book. But, on the very first page, he is quick to underline the fact that "the social processes do not fully explain the meaning of Christian life in the Church." [5] But, alas, out in the provinces among many literate and thoughtful Christian people, the social processes suffice,

[5] *Treasure in Earthen Vessel* (New York: Harper & Row, 1961), p .9.

if not to explain the Christian life, certainly to explain the church. It is a cultural, sociological phenomenon, and if there is a vertical dimension in its life—a ladder between man and God—the traffic is all one way, from man to God.[6] It is widely supposed that the initiative creative of church is man's. Man is the constructor. So even as the social sources of denominationalism can be traced, so can the church be adequately explained and satisfactorily described, it is claimed, without any concern for that dimension in its institutional and corporate life which transcends purely human categories. This meager and anthropocentric view of the church exists implicitly, even among many devout and reverent folk who take no such anthropocentric view of their own religious experience. There is an *ecclesiastical* humanism even among believers who have long since deserted any such simple and superficial humanism in personal religion.

It is my conviction that one of the causes for this ecclesiastical humanism among liberal Protestants lies in our vain neglect in this century of the Old Testament. The fragmentation of Christian faith, tragically symbolized by printing and distributing the Psalms and

[6] This figure of speech about the direction of the traffic between God and man does not apply when common attitudes about public worship are considered. Indeed, quite to the contrary. It is assumed that we go to church to get something from God, an attitude which may have more to do with the apparent irrelevance of much public worship than all the bad music and poor preaching in Christendom. Is it not curious that when we leave what we presume to call "our services," we ask our neighbor on the church steps the question, "Did you *get* anything out of church today?"

New Testament as the Scripture of the church, has had this grievous consequence. The parallel teaching that Pentecost is the birthday of the church, ignoring the concept of the new Israel, has sustained this view that the church and the Christian faith can be appropriated and understood without any reference to the Old Testament. The dictum of thirty years ago, that you turned to the Old Testament for texts on social religion and to the New Testament for texts on personal religion, is manifestly unfair to both the Old Testament and the New, but it hints at the truth presupposed in the Old Testament that the community of faith is God's creation and not man's devising. So the New Testament words of First Peter 2 are the words of Exodus 19: "You are a chosen race, a royal priesthood, a holy nation, God's own people, that you may declare the wonderful deeds of him who called you out of darkness into his marvelous light." (vs. 9.) So seriously have we neglected the Old Testament, and so completely have we lost the sense of the church as the community of the new covenant, that in many quarters the church is regarded as optional in the Christian life. No longer the elect, but the electing.

There is no minister in the provinces unacquainted with the absurdities thus fostered and the sacrilege thus encouraged. So the faithful seek the world's great to adorn the church, and generous supporters of the parish are not stewards of God but patrons of Jesus Christ. Yet more tragic than this is the widespread denial of the one community which transcends the ordinary basis of community, and thus could endure even for a nation on wheels. The reality of this community has been sacrificed to an illusory individualism sustained in religion, despite the wars, despite John Donne, despite taxation.

The distortion of Protestant church life, which ensues when community is ignored, is reflected in many of our public ceremonies, including the widely accepted spectator attitude in public worship. We borrow the phrase "to make my communion," and thereby suggest a highly individual act which is a far cry from a supper, and in which the passing of the elements among the "members" of the church is a distraction. We think that Sunday morning worship is called "public worship" because it is open to the public, and seldom do we realize that it is an act done in public as a public witness. In such an atomistic concept of the church, the issue of public responsibility in the witness of worship is no longer relevant, and it is reasonable to contend that whether or not one attends church is his own personal business. It also then follows that the minister who urges church attendance is promoting himself, for the congregation is a voluntary audience who has come to hear him and may legitimately dare him to hold its interest.

In similar strain, infant baptism is not a declaration of faith and an action of the whole church and an acceptance of responsibility by God's own people but at best a dedication of a child to God—giving God what is already God's—and at worst an occasion for a backyard cocktail party; marriage banns are unheard of;

and the burying ground around the parish church is a sweet but far too expensive anachronism surrendered to the real estate developer. All this is well known and widely lamented by the clergy, but here, as elsewhere, the gap between the clergy and the laity is wide—as wide as the gulf between the clear, practical implications of biblical faith in the parish church and the actual practice. Baptism is still something "done," often in private, a formalism or a magic; the clergy still substitute for the civil magistrate in marriages, adding some religious hokum and sentimentality; status or economics rather than faith still largely dictates funeral practice.[7]

However, not only is the sense of special divine community lost when the church is viewed as of man's contriving and presented as incidental to the Christian life;

[7] In our parish we have discovered genuine interest on the part of most parents when we have required that they attend a one-hour class for instruction in the meaning of infant baptism at least a week before presenting their children for the sacrament. We have also incorporated into the service itself a brief introduction explaining the sacrament, and have emphasized congregational participation. The introduction is a brief paraphrase of Bernard Manning's comments about baptism quoted by Dr. John Marsh in his Introduction to *A Book of Public Worship* (London: Oxford University Press, 1949). Much is being written elsewhere about funeral customs. It occurs to me that with the increasing acceptance of cremation, the parish church might consider the possibility of establishing a suitable place in or about church property for a simple columbarium. In regard to the religious customs and requirements of the marriage ceremony, the clergy is freer to salvage Christian meaning since there is ordinarily no commercial "middle man" intruding into the pastoral relationship. When a university student said to me recently, "You sure have to get a long way out of this town to find a preacher who will marry you in a hurry," I decided the churches in our community were making some progress in the reformation of marriage customs.

the loss is greater than that or possesses much more serious implications. Again, the loss is directly connected with a casual or contemptuous attitude toward the Old Testament. For when God is understood only as the Creator in general, the Great Original, the Mysterious Artificer, and is not embraced as the Creator in particular of a specific community, in a specific time and place, abstract and propositional theology tends to dominate the intellectual and spiritual life of the church, and the vigor and reality of biblical theology which takes human history seriously as an instructor in the Divine will and purpose is left behind. Indeed, abstract and propositional theology can be a hiding place from the reality of God's present activity in history, both personal and public. When we properly disabused our people of belief in a god who hunts up lost umbrellas, we may have also disabused them of faith in the God who reveals himself in his inescapable judgments in personal and public history. We have followed the first rule of philosophy which Langdon Gilkey claims "requires us to cease talking of God as a personal being, 'separate' from the universe, . . . and to begin to talk of God and the world as impersonal realities, mutually implying one another and so essentially related to one another." [8] Such a rule may be philosophy's enabling act, but it is the church's statute of limitation. Such innocuous religion would not be able to raise its head beyond the cultural societies and the philosophical sects and into the church at all, if the church remembered that it

[8] *Op. cit.*, p. 19.

is God's creation; this is an affirmation which cannot be casually overlooked, as one might overlook some interesting but incidental event in ancient history, if the Old Testament is included in the Scripture which we are to read, mark, and inwardly digest.

The celebration of Easter as a spring festival may symbolize the worst corruption of the best and the gravest distortion of Christian faith. Again, cannot this fundamental and fearful distortion be traced in part to the neglect or misunderstanding of the Old Testament? Alan Richardson writes:

> The faith of Israel, as Elijah and the prophets well knew, has nothing at all to do with the mythology of the Canaanite Baal. On the contrary, it is *historical* religion, and the characteristic feature of its great festivals is the commemoration of the saving acts of God in Israel's history, not the solemnization of the rebirth of nature. If God is known as the Lord of nature, this is because he has already been encountered as the Lord of history; and if the great festivals of Israel's liturgical year are still related to the seasons of nature, they have been altogether transformed by having been made the eschatological memorials of God's salvation in history.[9]

It is only as we review the mischief which follows our proud reluctance to accept God's revelation of himself in history and his special creative action in Israel—old and new—that we begin to sense the meaning of James Denny's dry comment. Denny once observed that the

[9] *Op. cit.,* pp. 138-39.

most serious difficulty to be contended with in a theological college is the divinity student who has previously obtained second-class honors in philosophy. Perhaps Denny could not bear to consider the difficulty the provincial church would encounter if that student were passed on from the school to the pulpit, largely untouched by the theological college. The provincial church in America unfortunately is prepared to describe that experience.

II

Consider now, if you will, a second area or cause of trouble in the provincial church—the watering down of God's love. There is evidence, I believe, that even when God is embraced as the active creating God, and the church is understood as his creation, the gospel of God's love has been so watered down as to provoke only superficial or trivial response. This is the heart-shaped religion given to us like a valentine to assure us that we are loved. Its perpetual text is the first phrase of John 3:16, which it keeps repeating over and over again like the Stainer anthem which cannot quite get off the ground. Or to phrase it differently, we have the appalling spectacle of a church offering God's love to his people as a helpful asset which they may put in their pockets and take home and find to be a friend indeed in some

37

time of need. Or again, this second trouble was described almost fifty years ago by P. T. Forsyth in his
lectures on a Christian theodicy. In 1916 he wrote, "The
religion of current society has come to a serious pass
and a day of judgment . . . because it has come to regard
God's love as the greatest asset of man instead of man's
trustful obedience as the supreme worship and due of
God." [10] Prophetic as Forsyth was, I doubt if he guessed
in his dreariest nights the incredible dilution and distortion of Christian faith which would come to pass
before another war would mark again the awfulness of
the majesty and the terror of the judgment that are
integral parts of the nature of God's love.

Again, the active creative God of history must be engaged against the god of the philosophers as he was engaged centuries ago by Lactantius, the Christian Cicero
of the fourth century, who claimed "that a God who
cannot be angry cannot love either: and a God that
knows neither love nor anger would [not be] the *living* God of Scripture." [11] The trouble in the province
which I report is not so much the absence of a sense of
God's judgment—that may actually be heightened in
these apocalyptic days—at least theoretically and ab-
stractly; the trouble is seen on the other side: the viewing of God's love as an asset to be embraced gratefully
and not as an incredible condescension prompting that

[10] *The Justification of God* (New York: Charles Scribner's Sons,
1917), p. 107.

[11] Rudolf Otto, *The Idea of the Holy* (London: Oxford University
Press, 1926), p. 100.

fear which is the beginning of wisdom and that love which is the source of obedience. The gospel of love as heard in the province does not have that sound. And the psalmist, were he quoted, "But there is forgiveness with thee, that thou mayest be feared" (Ps. 130:4), would be explained away. I am not getting ready to engage in another attack on the peace-of-mind cult in American Protestantism. Quite to the contrary, I am beginning to wonder if many of us who have relished participation in such attacks should not recognize the possibility that the peace-of-mind cult was trivializing the love of God openly and obviously, while we were doing the same thing secretly under the guise of theological sophistication. Did we simply engage in another form of the "heavenly utilitarianism" and "transcendental egoism" so deplored by Berdyaev.[12]

For example, we have quite rightly revived in our preaching and teaching the doctrine of justification by faith. How gratefully did we receive the words of Paul Tillich in the Terry Lectures, assuring us that "the courage to be is the courage to accept oneself as accepted in spite of being unacceptable." [13] So we returned to our parishes and our pulpits rejoicingly, like the shepherd who had found his lost sheep. We had at least found out how to find him, with the assistance of a highly honored theological trinity—Tillich, Luther, and Paul. But did we return to declare again the majesty

[12] Nicolas Berdyaev, *The Destiny of Man* (New York: Charles Scribner's Sons, 1937), p. 147.

[13] *The Courage To Be* (New Haven: Yale University Press, 1952), p. 164.

and the judgment and the incredible wonder of the love of God in Christ, and thus bring ourselves and our people trembling and fearful to our knees? Scarcely; we returned with a renewed nostrum for our anxiety. And although we called it an existential anxiety and sensed that much more was involved than curing peptic ulcers, nonetheless we preached what was essentially a peace of mind—that is, utilitarian, man-centered theology. Sophisticated, respectable, intellectual, but nonetheless trivial, because still anthropocentric. We came with an answer to a question, the asking of which we did not know how to prompt or which we feared to prompt, and thus paraded around Christendom presenting the spectacle of the boy who pulled out the plum, the essence of the pudding, to be sure, but only declared, "What a big boy am I."

So the second trouble followed fittingly upon the first, for this faith still matched the concept of the church as man's devising, or so we interpreted it. It was then at least consistent for us to plead with our people that if God in Christ thus accepts us, unacceptable as we are, and the church is Christ's body (our model of it, anyway), then the church must be a community of acceptance. And our people, bless them, rushed about trying to be accepting, and felt guilty when they could not manage it. Of course, it is true that the parish church ought to be a community of acceptance—but no "ought" makes it so. By this route it is not effected, because it is still self-serving; it is still man-centered; it is still, God help us, utilitarian. There is no man, living or dead, who can truly accept his neighbor apart from the fearful wonder of the experience and knowledge of his own incredible acceptance by God. We expected the benefits of Pauline theology, without the rigors of the Damascus Road; we yearned for the freedom of the confiding faith of Luther, without the gulfs and abysses of his experience, from which he fled for refuge to "the 'Word' like a hare to his cleft in the rocks." [14]

We have not been entirely unaware of our dilemma. Indeed, we have been more deeply aware than ever before that there was something in Christianity which we did not possess. So the search was intensified, and yet the genuine trouble in the parish church deepened. Its deepening was symbolized by the substitution of the study group for the prayer meeting. Sometimes this magnificent God, who still acts in history and still creates his church, tries to get through to us some hint of our trouble by sending an AA group to pray in the Sunday-school room while the office-bearers study in the church. The church out in the province was often supported in this earnest but tragic evasion of the risen Lord by the elder statesmen in the national offices of the denominations who would lend money to new congregations if they would put up the educational wing of an horrendous thing known as the "church plant" first.

Was it thus that the same fate which Rudolf Otto claims overcame the Lutheran revival was prepared for the faithful people out in the provinces to whom the

[14] Otto, *op. cit.*, p. 102.

postwar generation of young ministers carried the exciting revival of the New Testament theology? It was Otto's contention that the Lutheran revival came with such emphasis on the conceptual doctrinal that the "Church became a school, and her communications, in truth, found a more and more contracted access to the mind, as Tyrrell has put it somewhere, 'through the narrow clefts . . . of the understanding.' " [15] This stands in sorry contrast to the words of Luther which might be well addressed to us. "I mightily fear that few or no colleges, monasteries, altars and offices of the Church are really Christian in our day; no, nor the special fasts and prayers on certain saints' days either. I fear, I say, that in all these we seek only our own profit." [16]

Perhaps we gain some further understanding of how narrow are those "clefts of the understanding" cited by Tyrrell, and how limited a response is prompted when faith is thus circumscribed by reason, if we inquire thoughtfully into the reported loss of momentum in the missionary movement diverted now, too largely it seems to me, into the life of its stepchild, the ecumenical movement.[17] That movement is a thrust of contemporary Protestantism full of promise, but also, as I shall subsequently maintain, full of peril, too: perils

[15] *Ibid.*, p. 112.

[16] *Works of Martin Luther*, Philadelphia Edition (Philadelphia: Muhlenberg Press, 1943) , II, 341.

[17] Lesslie Newbigin, *One Body, One Gospel, One World* (London: Wm. Carling & Co., 1958) .

most keenly to be observed out in the provinces, where the need for a united body of Christ is a practical and daily need, and yet where it is becoming uncomfortably clear how willing the contemporary church is to sacrifice her holiness on the altar of her catholicity. The narrowness of the cleft of the understanding is also demonstrated by the ineffectuality which characterizes the ethical judgments of the prophetic movement in the church when they are separated from the *mysterium tremendum* of the energizing Cross, separated from the God there exposed and his silent demand for obedience as the absolute certification of adoration, its mark of authenticity. So Berdyaev suggests our ethics and morality will only be clear enough for action when we are no longer shut up in self-centeredness. "We must see the centre of being not in ourselves but in God, where it truly is, and then everything will fall into its right place." [18]

The missionary movement and the ecumenical movement, if they are now joined, as well as the prophetic movement of the church, must join with the whole church of Christ in remembering afresh the words of Evelyn Underhill a quarter of a century ago when she reminded us that each choice which the Christian makes, "each exercise of his limited freedom will either glorify or not glorify God; therefore he cannot divorce faith from works, or adoration from ethics." [19] Yet have we

[18] *Op. cit.,* p. 149.
[19] *Worship* (New York: Harper & Row, 1937), p. 79.

not all been witnesses of and participants in this disas-
trous separation? The history of some American denominations and their missionary personnel, social actionists,
ecumenists, and local ministers, from the Wall Street
crash to the first Eisenhower inauguration, is the history
of idealists motivated by Christian ethical insights who
took the missionary and prophetic task of the church
seriously. Yet it is a history which ended again and again
with either one of two equally tragic final chapters. One
of those chapters is headed "disillusionment," and tapers
off pathetically with a recital of the last days of the ideal-
ist consumed in writing a defense of ethical culture
or in embracing a well-heeled but reputedly "purely
spiritual" fundamentalism, or simply selling clergy signs
for automobiles from parsonage to parsonage. The al-
ternate final chapter is headed "fanaticism," and details
the newfound glory of the newfound party—communist
or John Birch, it makes little difference. Ethics divorced
from adoration! Christian ethics separated from the
Christian religion!

The same fate may await many enthusiastic supporters of and participants in the Peace Corps, which has
been widely described, especially by defensive missionary boards, as a modern missionary movement. Now
the Peace Corps is a very hopeful and valuable and creative response to a world marked by estrangement and
misunderstanding, but it is not a missionary movement
in the Christian sense, because like many social action
proposals it is primarily motivated by a reasonable ex-

pectation of some success.[20] Certainly conspicuous failure, such as Protestant missions suffered in China, would
undermine its motivation and close down its funds.
Failure would also make its secular supporters vulnerable to disillusionment or fanaticism. "A strategy of
brotherhood," wrote Reinhold Niebuhr in the midst of
the Second World War, "which has no other resource
but historical experience degenerates from mutuality
to a prudent regard for the interests of the self; and
from the impulse towards community to an acceptance
of the survival impulse as ethically normative." [21] But
the Christian missionary movement and the Christian
social action concern possess in their original temper—
that is, when they are unseparated from the adoration
of God—the resources to be magnificently indifferent
to the interests of the self, and have shown forth in every
century that new creation to which the survival impulse
is no longer relevant. Their primary motivation is not

[20] We have encouraged many of our parishioners to serve in the
Peace Corps and will continue to do so. Most of them understand the
distinction here emphasized. It is important that participating Christians understand this distinction.

If it is true, as some observers contend, that a general Protestant-
Catholic-Jew synthesis has taken place and produced an American
religion, I suppose it follows that the Peace Corps is its Missionary
Society. That is doubtless some improvement over the American religion whose missionaries are economic exploiters, save that their
contention as Christian evangelists is far easier to expose even if more
difficult to transform.

[21] *The Nature and Destiny of Man* (New York: Charles Scribner's
Sons, 1941), II, 96.

the promise of success but the cross of Jesus Christ.[22] They do as they are directed as an act of responsible obedience to God. So William J. Wolf writes and, significantly, not in a treatise on missions or social action but in a study of the Atonement: "The believer . . . can accept the frustration of his hopes because he knows that no line of activity undertaken in obedience to God's commands will ultimately be meaningless. . . . Man can be saved from the twin perils of disillusionment and of fanaticism by the redemptive power of the Cross." [23]

We have been so keen, and rightfully so, to follow with integrity and courage the social and public and churchly implications of our faith, that we have overlooked or bypassed or, more, backed away from the profoundly personal nature of God's representation of himself to us, however social and public and outward is the essential instrument, his church. The social nature of the instrument of encounter may obscure for us its demandingly personal implications. Who of us has not hedged at this point, does not hedge? Why is it that we still smile at the mention of Jonathan Edwards' famous Enfield sermon, "Sinners in the Hands of an

[22] When our parish first began work with parolees from prison, we were warned that if we expected any very high percentage of success we would soon grow weary with waiting. Without some other motivation this work would fall by the wayside. Is that one reason it has received so pitifully little attention over the years? See Chap. III for report of actual parish involvement in prisoner rehabilitation.

[23] *No Cross, No Crown* (Garden City, N. Y.: Doubleday & Co., 1957), p. 157.

Angry God," [24] and earnestly persuade ourselves that God's love for his creation does not include anger and cannot provoke fear? But even if it can and should and does, we comfort ourselves with the thought of the community of faith or faithlessness; after all, are we not all in this together? There is not one spider on the end of that slender filament, my dear Jonathan, but hundreds! We remember the corporate nature of the faith and of the church and quote John Donne again reassuringly and remember the solidarity of the new Israel. True, true, but did you read Arthur Miller's essay on juvenile delinquency in a recent issue of *Harper's Magazine?* Do you remember the strange spectacle he reported watching with amazement one afternoon while on an outing with a tough urban gang? "In the afternoon," he writes, "we started a baseball game, and everything proceeded normally until somebody hit a ball to the outfield. I turned to watch the play and saw ten or twelve kids running for the catch. It turned out that not one of them was willing to play the outfield by himself, insisting that the entire group hang around out there together. The reason was that a boy alone might drop a catch and would not be able to bear the

[24] It is interesting in this context to note that this famous sermon which caused such a stir when preached in Enfield, Connecticut, on July 8, 1741, had been preached the previous month to Edwards' own congregation in Northampton apparently without exceptional response. Parish ministers may well note that when a revival came to *that* congregation, it was provoked by a series of sermons on the divine love in Christ based on First Corinthians 13. Cf. R. G. Turnbull, *Jonathan Edwards the Preacher* (Grand Rapids: Baker Book House, 1958), pp. 100 ff.

humiliation. So they ran around out there in a drove all afternoon, creating a stampede every time a ball was hit." [25] *There* is the corporate nature of the church and human life for you—creating a "togetherness-stampede" every time a ball is hit! But no one can catch the ball for you, and no one can die for you, and no one can face the Cross for you, and God's love is not something to take home in your pocket to pull out for a comfortable feeling of acceptance, but a blinding, dazzling light calling for an individual response of faith and obedience. It is a case of religious malnutrition when the hungry sheep are fed week after week various combinations of the Twenty-third Psalm and John 14, where there is no preaching of the utter and indescribable holiness of God, no preaching of a gospel which placards the Cross and reaches for words and past words into actions—the actions of breaking and pouring to reenact so cleanly and so plainly the gracious, demanding holiness of God, so cleanly and so plainly that even he who runs, runs from it to the study group or the Peace Corps or the Social Action Committee, may read it and reading it be filled with the human response to holiness which is humility.

So it was with that woman of the city who was stopped in her running by the presence of Christ and who brought an alabaster flask of ointment to anoint his feet as he sat at the table with the Pharisees. And thinking of her, Paul Tillich writes, "We are suddenly grasped by the certainty that we are forgiven, and the fire of

[25] "The Bored and the Violent," November, 1962, p. 52.

love begins to burn. That is the greatest experience anyone can have. It may not happen often, but when it does happen, it decides and transforms everything." [26] The issue of this experience is the possession of a humility of a sort which Berdyaev says "always means the acquisition of greater freedom. . . . Man must be inwardly free even if he happens to be a slave." [27] "For freedom Christ has set us free" (Gal. 5:1, RSV) Paul wrote, and then in the same epistle protested, "O you stupid Galatians . . . you must have been bewitched— you before whose eyes Christ was openly displayed upon his cross!" (Gal. 3:1, NEB).

Perhaps it is only as we lend ourselves to the worship and adoration of God for his own sake that we will come to understand how truly narrow are "the clefts of the understanding." Indeed, it may be the search for answers to our ethical dilemmas which will prompt the long overdue reformation of Protestant worship, a reformation to be centered not so much in outward form (the forms are still there to be filled with meaning) as in the expectations of the inner man, and to be fulfilled not so much in liturgical purity as in an ethical spontaneity. As C. H. Dodd puts it in his introduction to Romans 12, Paul "does not think of right conduct either as conformity with a code or as the adding of virtue to virtue in a discipline of self-culture. It is the *harvest of the Spirit*—a spontaneous reaction of the in-

[26] *The New Being* (New York: Charles Scribner's Sons, 1955) , p. 13.
[27] *Op. cit.*, p. 150.

ward spirit of a man, controlled by the Spirit of God, to the successive situations in which he finds himself as he lives with other men in society." [28]

The temptation is to enter a few paragraphs at this point about the dreadful state of public worship in liberal Protestantism, but its inadequacy is implicit in every serious trouble plaguing the church today. Its reform will not be achieved by tampering with the mechanics, or even by renewing the forms, but by stripping away every "bewitchment" which shades our eyes, like the eyes of the Galatians, from that open display upon the Cross. Any remedy short of this central confrontation may be another attempt to hide the seriousness of our plight. In seeking the renewal of worship through new modes and methods, or rearrangement of old ones, reminds me of the observation of Lloyd J. Averill about problems in marriage. "When in marriage two people find that something is lacking in the physical aspect of their relationship, they are likely to turn to the marriage manuals to find out what has gone wrong with their technique. But all the technique in the world cannot fill the emptiness which grows between two people who no longer have anything important to say to each other." [29] Is this the vacancy which the troubles in the parish churches of the Protestant world declare?

[28] *The Epistle of Paul to the Romans* (New York: Harper & Bros., 1932), pp. 188-89.
[29] "Sexuality in Crisis," *The Christian Century*, October 2, 1963, p. 1198.

III

This suggestion that the emptiness in public worship may arise from a basic emptiness in the conversation between God and man brings us abruptly and squarely before the third area of trouble in the ordinary parish church. At least it is a grievous trouble in churches with an educated ministry and a critical view of the Scriptures. That trouble can scarcely be identified as "trouble," for "trouble" is a word to describe a failure which carries within it the potential of catastrophe, personal and public. That failure, I believe, is just this: That the single, unique, objective gospel that the Almighty, transcendent, everliving, Creator God invaded human history in Jesus Christ to deliver man from sin and death is seldom proclaimed in such fashion that it can be heard even where it is affirmed, because the human situation to which it is addressed is hidden or denied even by the church itself. The conversation is empty, because men do not know or admit they know what God is talking about. Thus, the gospel is actually proclaimed irrelevantly, because even in this apocalyptic age we continue to hide from the ultimate religious problem, the problem of evil. This failure effectively eliminates both incarnation and atonement, no matter how ardently those affirmations and their associated doctrines are elaborated theologically and liturgically or how passionately the Cross is elevated and declared crucial to the faith. The unique reconciling power of the faith enshrined in those doctrines and placarded in that Cross can only be heard both in the mind and in the heart by those who have been confronted seriously with the problem of evil and awakened to its actual measure. The redeeming answer prepared from the foundation of the world cannot be heard when the question inherent in the corruption of that foundation has not been asked. Furthermore, the constant and creative tension between faith and doubt, in which the church as preacher holds the answer, would not dismay if we more rigorously exposed the question: that is, prompted it, prepared it, decked it out with all the color of an atomic sky and all the anguish of the stern heroism which freedom demands in the heart of one who loves.

In an essay on "Existentialist Aspects of Modern Art," Paul Tillich suggests that the churches have followed the bourgeoisie resistance to modern art because they believed they had all the answers to life.

But in believing they had all the answers they deprived the answers of their meaning. These answers were no longer understood because the questions were no longer understood, and this was the churches' fault. They did not do what the existentialist artist did. They did not ask the questions over again as they should have out of the experience of despair in industrial society. The churches did not ask the question, and therefore their answers, all the religious answers Christianity has in its creeds, became empty.[30]

[30] *Christianity and the Existentialists,* ed. Carl Michalson (New York: Charles Scribner's Sons, 1956), p. 146.

Dorothy L. Sayers presses the same indictment in many of her works. Indeed, she seeks to provoke the right questions. She maintains that the "incapacity for asking the right question has grown, in our time and country, to the proportions of an endemic disease." [31]

It is not necessary to study an elaborate theodicy to face the dimension of this problem, although is it not instructive that D. C. Macintosh, professor of systematic theology at Yale between World Wars I and II, entered his ordered essay on the problem of evil as an appendix to his basic work, *Theology as an Empirical Science?* However, no exposition of a rational theodicy is necessary. All that is required is the sensitivity to see that that which distresses us in all the pain and anguish and unfulfillment of creation, as Oliver Quick made so clear, is "that our moral sense is outraged." This is in truth the nature of our rebellion and our hurt; this is the nature of our reaction to all the senseless waste and painful incompletion we see and experience. It is there to be felt in the cruel children on the playground tormenting the child who is different, and thus early revealing afresh the egoistic corruption of human existence; it is there to resent and resist in the ravages of disease, both in body personal and in body politic, inner melanoma and outward malefaction. Without profound realism about the nature of evil, the relevance of the gospel with Christ "openly displayed upon his cross" cannot come into focus; and that realism may begin on

[31] *The Mind of the Maker* (Living Age ed. New York: Meridian Books, 1956), p. 175.

the playground or in the therapist's chamber, both the X-ray therapist and the psychotherapist, when we recognize that "it is truer to say that the world is painful and distressing to us, because it appears to be immoral, than to say that it appears to us to be immoral because it is painful and distressing." [32]

The Christian message, good news, can scarcely be heard by those who are asleep to this basic religious question. The cry, "Sleepers, awake," must go before and accompany the proclamation of the Cross. This is the primary evangelistic problem—to provoke the right question. D. T. Niles quotes a friend who has put the evangelistic problem in a striking parable:

A sleepwalker may safely cross a chasm by the narrowest of shaking planks. He is too absorbed in his dream to realize the full threat of the gulf beneath. But let him wake and he will fall. Now in soul and conscience men are prone to be as inappreciative as the sleepwalker of the abysses they think to pass. But when once Christ has stirred them to wakeful perception of the engulfing depths that divide the guilty conscience from trust in God's liberty and readiness to forgive, then by no other bridge than His Cross can they win again to "joy and peace in believing." [33]

When I first read that I thought, why then disturb the sleepwalker at all? Ignorance is bliss! But tragically

---

[32] Oliver C. Quick, *Doctrines of the Creed* (New York: Charles Scribner's Sons, 1938), pp. 198, 200.

[33] *That They May Have Life* (London: Lutterworth Press, 1952), p. 13.

enough and in truth that is the conclusion many of us have reached, and yet it is one which can be reached only by those who have never been awakened from either sleep or ignorance, who have not loved or been loved.

To claim that the gospel is not heard because the actual human situation to which it is addressed is hidden or denied is not to say that our generation is unaware of the tragic in life. Perhaps it is more aware than any recent generation has been; but it is often a superficial awareness, one which prompts dismay or rebellion or tears or "God-is-dead" art and literature, an awareness that escapes into old disharmonies and new dishonesties but never probes deeply enough or objectively enough to be provoked into repentance. It is an awareness which may prompt a Wellesley historian to expound, according to the *New York Times,* 310 pages of the theory that "the colossal world crisis facing twentieth century man can be resolved only by vigorous total commitment to an organic world civilization . . . with a new world synthesis of cultures, philosophies, political systems, economies and religions." [34] It is an awareness sufficiently worrisome and provocative to send men hustling to other modern religions, the physical sciences to eliminate outward threats, psychoanalysis to eliminate inward threats, and to Utopian faith in human progress to ease threats of ultimate meaninglessness, but not sufficiently sensitive to see that these substitute or supple-

[34] Review of *The City of Man* by W. W. Wager, *New York Times,* April 5, 1963.

mentary or partial religions and their fruit are *also* subject to sin and its chief servant, death.[35]

In the midst of these new and helpful but finite dependencies, we have not sufficiently recognized that should they redeem us from outward conflicts and inner chaos, from the fetters of social injustice and the restrictive power of inner distortions and sickness—should we get East Harlem cleaned up and racial justice in Berkeley flowing like a mighty stream—should our emotional conflicts be so resolved that we could love and be loved, should all this come about, the gospel could not even then be stored away as a relic for examination in the archives of some Parliament of Man. It could not be so shelved because, with these outward distractions removed,[36] the problem of evil would press all the more acutely in its cleanest, sharpest form: that is the contradiction, the tragic element within love itself, unresolved and intolerable if the Cross be mere martyrdom, even the grandest, most sublime instance of martyrdom. Although the eternally tragic element in life is expressed through social forms (the children on the playground), and in physical forms (disease and storms), it exists independently of them. The deepest tragedy may not be after all in unrequited love but in love that is returned and in its return imposes demands of a higher obedience and reveals a more profound law—namely, that perfect love is not victorious *over* death at all but is victorious

[35] Cf. Langdon Gilkey, *op. cit.*

[36] Berdyaev claimed that "man's liberation from social forms which oppress and enslave him . . . puts before him the moral and religious problem in its pure form." *Op. cit.*, p. 201.

only *through* death! [37] The trouble in the parish church of the liberal, emancipated, literate type which is hereby reported for clarification and correction through the theological disciplines, both theological and practical, is not the trouble of thirty years ago—the preaching of a gospel of little consequence—but the preaching of a very great gospel with little consequence, because the problem, the only problem of significance, to which it is relevant and to which it is addressed is hidden or denied. Every Easter morning we dramatize this trouble as we proclaim good news to those who have not considered the bad news, as we preach the Resurrection to those who do not know they are participants in the Crucifixion!

[37] Quick, *op. cit.*, chap. 20.

II

THE CHURCH ASSEMBLED

In his study of Jeremiah, Adam Welch claimed that Jeremiah was able to sense the troubles that plagued the old Israel because he did not belong to the professional priesthood, and thus was free of the narrowness which creeps over the official caste. Jeremiah, Welch claimed, was not working from the inside, and thus was able to command a broader and more objective view. There are many critics of the conventional parish church abroad in our day who do not belong to the official priesthood, and who claim Jeremiah's privileged point of view. Indeed, occasionally such a critic is a member of the faculty or the student body of a theological school. Often, however, he fools himself about his objectivity, and in his jeremiads one hears not so much the cool, detached critique of the outsider, but the neurotic response of the disguised insider who has never recovered from the trauma provoked by compulsory Sunday-school attendance as an adolescent. The reputed objectivity of any such pseudo-Jeremiah is not trustworthy, for like everyone else who knows the name of Jesus Christ, he also is beholden to the church. Indeed, his embarrassment may stem from that fact, and shake it as he may, and deny it as he will, and separate himself from it as he does, he can never escape the truth that he cannot now ever really be outside the church; someone else has already seen to that. Perhaps it was his old Aunt Margaret who unwittingly conveyed apostolic succession,[1] or the secular community with its public libraries and public schools—perhaps even God himself. His existence within the church may be only as a heckler or parasite or detractor, but exist there he does. For that he may one day give profound thanks to

[1] "The Work of Christ is perpetuated only in the Church of Christ. To adopt an emendation of the children's hymn:

> Jesus loves me, this I know
> For my mother tells me so.

If the doctrine of Apostolic Succession means anything which excludes this, it is out of line with the only historic realities which matter." J. S. Whale, *Christian Doctrine* (New York: Cambridge University Press, 1952), p. 128.

God, for there still is no salvation outside the church, although even within it we may continue our estrangement from God.

I

While leaving the question of salvation open with seemly modesty, no parish minister can presume Jeremiah's stance in his critique of the church. Now it may be true, as Adam Welch claimed, that there is a professional narrowness and subjectivity in the clergy as a caste; it is also true that every Christian is of the church, and when we are moved to report its troubles it may be well to be cautioned by the somewhat inelegant observation that "it is a foul bird who besmears his own nest." So I am moved to maintain that although, as I have suggested in the preceding chapter, there is much to trouble us in the conventional parish church, there is new life and hope, too. Some of this new life is breaking forth, as you know, in those places where the church has courageously embraced, or been compelled to embrace, radical change—quiet, painful, sacrificial—issuing in new life. Especially since World War II some of the most gifted and promising young Protestant clergymen have moved into the sorriest sections of many great American cities to nurture the church and bring it to new vitality in natural and relevant forms. In some instances this work in the troubled provinces of the inner city has helped spark magnificent outward re-newal of the city, and less dramatically has been an in-strument to disclose unsuspected hidden grandeur in some very ordinary human persons.

There are other radical breaks with conventional methods and organizational assumptions in American Protestantism which are signs of hope. Some of these new commitments are in response to new needs and structures in society, and others are the alternatives pro-posed and followed by those who are in despair over the faithlessness and apostasy of the ordinary middle-class provincial church. Although no one who loves Christ, as well as his church, could fail to share much of the anguish of those who have given up the conven-tional church as lost, all of us might well remember that now, as in the past, it is the ordinary, prosaic parish church that has somehow managed to preserve and per-petuate the very standards by which it is judged and found wanting. If it is true that the church in its "true being" protests against the church in its expression,[2] is it not also true that this protesting "true being" exists primarily in the corrupted expression against which it protests?

Churchmen laboring out in the provinces of America today could well read again a book by Roland Allen published in 1927 entitled *Missionary Methods, St. Paul's or Ours, A Study of the Church in the Four Provinces.* The title suggests a pertinency which does not disappoint us. Mr. Allen maintains, for example,

[2] Suggested by Paul Tillich in the Earl Lectures, 1963.

that Paul went where the Spirit led, sought open doors, and "chose the centres most suitable for the gathering of converts and the propagation of the faith." If we follow those methods, some of us may be led back to the much-maligned conventional church. It may be that God in his creative wisdom has preserved these traditional forms for some good purpose. Harry Emerson Fosdick was critical of traditional forms forty years ago in a fashion that opened the way for the renewal of a biblical theology beyond his own reckoning—a fact some contemporary and competent biblical theologians tend to overlook altogether. Critical as Fosdick was of lifeless forms, yet he told the story of the College of William and Mary which was damaged and closed during the Civil War. Precariously it was reopened afterward, and then faced the necessity of another suspension which lasted seven years.

"But 'every morning,' we read, 'during those seven barren years President Ewell rang the chapel bell. There were no students; the faculty had disappeared; and rain seeped through the leaky roofs of the desolate buildings. But President Ewell still rang the bell.' . . . He was keeping up the form, as though to say, Despite immediate disaster, the intellectual life will come back again and fill these empty halls with reality once more and be a vital and dynamic power. More than once in history the church has done that." [3]

[3] *A Great Time To Be Alive* (New York: Harper & Bros., 1944), pp. 96-97.

Although it is presumptuous to suggest that the forms inherent to the parish church have been preserved until *our* generation could get here to fill them again with force, is it not also presumptuous to suggest that we can safely ignore these forms and write them off as hopeless anachronisms? Richard Niebuhr reminded us that "the 'big operator' represents a perversion of the minister's office, not because he is an executive but because he does not administer the Church's work." [4] Can the church's work be done in and through the conventional parish church—even one which requires the minister to be a button-pushing executive, or is it so hindered by its wall-to-wall carpets and its identification with American middle-class mores that a radical break must be made and new forms must be found if the old force is to be entertained?

In the preparation of a sermon it is a fair and proper homiletical device not to disclose what point three is going to be until you have labored through point two, and to save point two until you have finished point one. This is a technique of suspense. However, this is not a sermon, and if you want to know the final point, you can leaf ahead and find it. Therefore, it makes sense to confess right here what you have already guessed— that this bird is not just about ready to besmear his own nest, and that he believes that the work of the church of God can yet be done in and through the conventional parish church. Furthermore, there is heartening

[4] *The Purpose of the Church and Its Ministry* (New York: Harper & Row, 1956), p. 81.

evidence that part of the purpose of God in encouraging some of the radical breaks with old forms, such as the severe conditions of membership imposed by the Church of the Saviour in Washington, D.C., or the patterns of discipline in daily life fostered by the Iona community and some inner-city group ministries, is not simply to sustain the immediate work of those particular groups but to reinvigorate the conventional church, which fortunately does not remain entirely unmoved by these witnesses. The principle of counterreformation abides, and there are some encouraging signs that the ordinary parish church is stirring with new life, camouflaged or channeled as it may be in old and familiar forms.

Before we consider some suggestions for the reinvigoration of the old forms, it is important to spell out the grave danger in which the church stands whenever the appointed and ordained ministry grows impatient with the people of the gathered parish and seeks to exercise its ministry directly to the world. Much of the weakness of American Protestantism rests in this misunderstanding of and impatience with the church on the part of the professional ministry and the consequent misdirection of energy. How easy it is for the parish minister, growing impatient with a dull and stiff-necked congregation, to bypass the congregation, and seek to exercise a ministry directly and personally and independently upon the world. I do not mean the kind of direct ministry which every Christian ought to exercise, clergyman and layman alike, but a special kind possessed of a presumed authority symbolized by a special title—and sometimes special dress. This is to short-circuit the church and is one of the frequently overlooked consequences of what Gustaf Aulén describes as the 'subjective misinterpretation" [5] of the ministry, wherein the minister's authority rests in his personal piety or in his presumed superiority as a critic and judge of specific ambiguous political and economic questions. He is responsible in these areas, but not omniscient, either by virtue of ordination or a theological degree. What incredible theological and moral gymnastics are required to hold simultaneously this subjective misinterpretation of the ministry and the doctrine of the priesthood of all believers! One suspects the fine work of the devil in this balancing act. The ministry of the church is the ministry of the whole church, of the entire people of God, not the ministry of the ordained clergy. The role of the ordained clergy is far less spectacular. Their ministry is *in* the church, and it is sustained as the essential gift of God to the church in order that the ministry *of* the church *to* the world may be exercised. The clergyman is appointed to nurture the church and to direct the church's ministry, not to exercise it personally in holy separation. This rule applies, it seems to me, even in his role as preacher, as we shall see in a moment, "for a Church with a history should not sink to be a mere rostrum for a reputation." [6]

[5] *The Faith of the Christian Church* (Philadelphia: Muhlenberg Press, 1948), pp. 413 ff.

[6] P. T. Forsyth, *The Church and the Sacraments* (London: The Independent Press, 1917), p. 149.

Could it be that the period of the great preachers of the nineteenth century, the period of the renowned "pulpiteers" with large "auditories," now viewed by some Protestants with great nostalgia, actually marked the beginning of decadence and decline in Protestantism rather than new vitality and power? Contemporary mass evangelism is doubtless supported by hundreds of sincere and earnest Christians, but even with the help of Madison Avenue an anachronism remains an anachronism! In his book *The Purpose of the Church and Its Ministry*, H. Richard Niebuhr developed the description of the contemporary minister as pastoral director. Many of us who were in conversation with him while he was writing that book remember how unhappy he was with that term, and we shared his distress over the number of people who took exception to the term without trying to understand his development of it. Now, eight years after that book was published, and after four years of personal reinvolvement in the actualities of the provincial church, I am impressed by the accuracy of his analysis. Professor Niebuhr wrote:

The pastoral director carries on all the traditional functions of the ministry—preaching, leading the worshiping community, administering the sacraments, caring for souls, presiding over the church. But as the preacher and priest organized these traditional functions in special ways so does the pastoral director. His first function is that of building or "edifying" the church; he is concerned in everything that he does to bring into being a people of **God** who as a

Church will serve the purpose of the Church in the local community and the world.[7]

In some churches the minister gives each new member a special text just for him when he joins the church. This sentimental practice can scarcely be defended, but God works as he pleases, and I have often thought that it would only be fair for each new member to respond by handing the minister a special text to remind *him* of *his* responsibility. An appropriate one might be Galatians 6:10: "Do good to all men, . . . especially to those who are of the household of faith." The minister as pastoral director bears this particular responsibility to those who are of the household of faith and must obey this particular charge. His complaints about the stiff-necked people in his care and the ineffectiveness of his parish in the world are suspect until he has stretched with earnest prayer every gift with which he has been endowed of intellect and imagination and love and physical health to stir his parish to exercise its ministry to the whole world. The minister bears primary responsibility to hold his own being open to and as a channel for the renewing activity of the Creator of the church, to provide the first instance of openness in the church "to the judging and renewing activity of the living God made known in Jesus Christ," an openness which Robert McAfee Brown claims to mark the spirit of Protestantism.[8]

[7] H. Richard Niebuhr, *op. cit.*, p. 82.

[8] *The Spirit of Protestantism* (New York: Oxford University Press, 1961) , p. 40.

If the ordained minister reviews and accepts this awesome responsibility as a pastoral director, the whole church may be renewed as he assists his particular people to look again more closely at the twofold nature of the life of the church, its inner life and its outer life, its nurture and its ministry. It has been widely and wisely said that the people of God come together in the church so they may go out into the world and be the church. This dramatic coming and going characterizes the lives of the people of God. It is the incarnated dialectic of the church's existence, its vital rhythm. Parenthetically, we may note that sickness in the local parish may be measured by the degree of imbalance between these two mutually dependent and complementary movements. When the church is all inner life, all "coming together," when the community of faith simply engages in the manicuring of its own soul, it has the sickness of obesity, indigestion, a permanent retreat of which the fat monk is the symbol; when it is all outer life, all "going out," action, drive, it has the sickness of malnutrition, emaciation, hardness, of which the worn-out social worker is the symbol. The minister, the pastoral director, is charged to maintain the balance, not to keep peace but to promote health and life. Let us consider the revival and reinvigoration of the traditional forms of the provincial church by looking at these two aspects of its life. In the balance of this chapter we will consider its coming together and in the next chapter its going out, the church assembled and the church dispersed.

II

The church's coming together is marked not only by groups organized for study or prayer, but also and eternally by committees, boards, the traditional and often time-consuming instrumentalities of its common life. However, when we talk about redemptive groups in the church, we seldom think of these groups. Yet, can a minister sit with the trustees, for example, through a discussion of the investment of an endowment fund or the consideration of rules for the use of the church kitchen and miss altogether the opportunity for the nurture of the inner life of the church? The minister may complain all the day long about the sickness with which the world has infected the church so that the position of trustee, one who supervises material things in the church, is more honored and coveted than the position of deacon or its equivalent, one who is responsible for the spiritual life of the church. He may be a better pastoral director, however, and less of a pastoral lamenter if he helps the parish recognize this sorry infection and understand its distortion, and perhaps even persuade the trustees to suggest to the whole church that no man be eligible for that board until he has served as a deacon, on the premise that such service is prerequisite to exercising a wise trusteeship. To inject such a consideration into the coming together of such a prosaic group in the church as the trustees might demonstrate how God still moves in mysterious ways his wonders to perform.

As we consider the church's coming together in committee and board and study and prayer groups, we see afresh the disaster which threatens the church which forgets the Old Testament and ignores the communal nature of the religion of the New Testament. We have emphasized the intimate aloneness of religious experience, and yet those tremendous moments of personal encounter, of private religion, do not come out of the blue; they come in and out of the church's coming together. Charles R. Brown may have called out, "What about St. Paul?" [9] when a Beecher Lecturer at Yale contended for the priority of the church in Christian experience, and earlier pages in this volume may have emphasized the essential loneliness of the Damascus Road; but it is also true that the women at the tomb, the preaching of Peter, and the stoning of Stephen came first. So the faith of the community of faith surrounds and orders the faith of individuals; indeed, may be the essential instrument for the delivery of that gift of faith. Lesslie Newbigin reminds us that

while faith is in general required of those upon whom Christ performs his mighty works of healing, it is clear that the faith of family and friends, the faith of a group, may be as important as or more important than that of the individual. The paralytic man is healed when Jesus sees the faith of his four friends, the centurion's servant in response

[9] Edgar DeWitt Jones, *The Royalty of the Pulpit* (New York: Harper & Bros., 1951), p. 237.

71

to the believing prayer of his master, and the Syro-Phoenician girl in response to that of her mother.[10]

One scarcely dares whisper this biblical witness in some quarters today for fear that the group therapist will take over the ministry of the church altogether; yet out in the parish churches we are discovering what happens sometimes in groups, in the coming together of the church. As an aside, may I suggest that the muffled sound of celestial laughter one occasionally hears high overhead, when small groups are presented as a new development in the life of the church, comes from some of our Methodist fathers who are holding an old-fashioned class meeting with John Wesley around the heavenly throne. A commission appointed to study the area of pastoral care in our particular parish spent many months considering the wisdom of establishing a church-centered psychological clinic. They were not content with the prospect, and somehow felt that the church might have more to offer than a pale imitation of an outpatient clinic under rent-free ecclesiastical auspices. As they continued their study they came to the conclusion that no plan of pastoral care which fundamentally ignored or bypassed the basic communal nature of the parish church could be satisfactory. They recognized the necessity for individual pastoral care and for continued referral and cooperation between the ministers and physicians and psychologists and social workers. Yet they emphasized the necessity for the ministers and

[10] *The Household of God* (New York: Friendship Press, 1954), p. 66.

lay leaders of the church to be trained and alert to direct all group life in the church, all coming together as a people of God, to be more effective instruments of pastoral care, to see that persons were more important than agenda, and that every group—as well as specially organized groups, such as Parents Without Partners and Alcoholics Anonymous—be sensitive to its potential as a means of healing and of hope. They said, in effect, the minister alone cannot lower the paralytic through the roof into the presence of Jesus. It takes his four friends and more.

I was attracted to an obscure scholarly monograph because its title intrigued me: "The Role of Sympathy in the Psychotherapeutic Process." [11] Although that paper revealed a presumptuous inadequacy in biblical theology, it also contained confirmation from the psychotherapist's point of view of the miracles which may take place in individual lives as they participate in the deepest part of the church's "coming together," which is not simply for mutual support and encouragement, but to open up a Damascus Road where God discloses himself and wins our free obedience. The writer reported, "We find greatest achievement in the endurance of suffering among those personalities who are committed and dedicated to goals beyond the limits of egocentricity." "Beyond the limits of egocentricity!"—my word! Is this not the response of obedience to the suffering Savior which is one way to describe the goal of all

[11] Edith Weigert, Ninth Annual Karen Horney Lecture, *Journal of Psychoanalysis*, XXII (1962), No. 1.

our coming together? This paper concluded, "Whether the *therapist* knows it or not, he lives his philosophy. It may radiate warmth and kindle the light of sympathetic understanding, which has an evocative, creative influence on the patient, not only convincing the intellect, but transforming the heart." One might exchange the word "therapist" for the word "minister." A few years ago that would have been my proposal, and I hope it still has validity. But how limited the range of that ministry! There is a widening which the substitution of the word "Christian person" suggests. Yet it is nearer the biblical truth and parish wisdom to substitute for "therapist" not the words "minister" or "Christian person," but the words "parish church" or "community of faith." Such a proposal finds support in many quarters; so "Heidegger calls the basic being-in-the-world a being-with-others, a caring for others, and being cared for by others." [12]

III

At once, however, the dangers of this potential new force in old forms present themselves. Among them is that fundamental danger, which we sought to suggest in the first chapter, of making God's love an asset and trivializing the doctrine of justification by faith by forgetting that the end of man is to glorify God and not

[12] Weigert, *op. cit.*

himself. Is there some practical method by which these dangers and the dangers of excessive subjectivism and self-centeredness in the group life of the church may be avoided? As we search for an answer to that question, we may observe that the "coming together" of the church not only involves the doctrine of justification by faith but is, as well, a practical illustration of the working out of that other classical Protestant doctrine of the priesthood of all believers. Certainly insofar as that doctrine underlines the responsibility of each Christian to be a priest to his brother, it is illustrated not only in passing the elements of the Lord's Supper from Christian to Christian in the pews, but also in all our coming together for mutual support and care. This observation does not in itself guard against the inherent dangers which concern us, but it points us to another Protestant affirmation which may—the authority of the Bible. If the Bible is the "infallible rule of faith and practice," does it help us in this dilemma?

We were considering this question in our parish while we were wrestling with the conviction that ordinarily preaching should not only be expository but also that preaching is properly a function of the entire church and not of one man. About this time we were led to Dietrich Ritschl's study of the nature of preaching, entitled *A Theology of Proclamation*. Ritschl supported our growing conviction that if the entire church were to engage in the ministry of the church, then it must somehow share responsibility with the minister for the preparation of the sermon.

In our parish we are experimenting with what is called a "sermon seminar," in an effort to bring these various concerns under an appropriate and creative discipline—"a coming together," in which the benefits of mutual support are directed by the unfolding of the Word and are specifically related to the "going out" of the whole church. Each Sunday's calendar carries the announcement of the text for the following Sunday or the lesson which the sermon will seek to open up— "expose." Then on Wednesday nights the entire congregation is invited to come to the church for a sermon seminar at 8:15 P.M. A small but significant remnant of the parish usually appears. The hour is late, to enable parents of young children to come more easily and also to discourage casual attendants. The first announcement of this meeting carried the admonition that this was not another "activity" of the church to be supported. We begin promptly at 8:15 P.M., and the minister who is to preach on the following Sunday does a brief nontechnical exegesis of the passage. The exegete tries to remove unnecessary obstacles to an understanding of the passage, but he tries to avoid purely technical questions which are not in themselves hazardous. For example, he would warn against the dangers of allegorizing certain parables, but he would not explain probable common sources unless that question appeared to him to bear with particular significance upon the meaning. The effort is to try to make as clear as possible the meaning and intent of the biblical writer. A lover need not worry about misspelling in a love note he receives, but he is necessarily perplexed when he cannot decipher even to whom the note is addressed. Nonetheless, the devil does sometimes attempt to derail us at this point by leading us into interesting speculation about some technical biblical question.

Following the exegesis the seminar divides into four or five groups of eight to ten each for forty minutes of discussion of the passage. Each group elects a leader, and it is widely announced that the ultimate in leadership in these groups is to get through the entire forty minutes without a word from the leader. Group dynamics par excellence! The groups are urged to follow the lead of the scripture, but to remember their own problems and questions of faith and life. The preacher sits in on one group, and later gets spontaneous reports from the other groups. He tries to listen and speaks only rarely and then in his role as the exegete. It is here that the congregation begins to prepare the sermon; but in the process witnessing and confession and doubting and support have taken place. Sometimes Christian discipline and rebuke have been experienced profitably; and in the sermon seminar care is always taken to see that each person is established as a person with a name, a critically important feature if we are to retain the genius of Protestant parish life in our large un-Protestant-sized churches. At 9:10 P.M. the groups reassemble in the larger seminar for a sentence or two of report and for fifteen minutes of prayer. The lesson just studied and discussed often is creative of the few brief spoken prayers that may be offered by members of the group.

Sometimes there is almost no spoken prayer at all, and on other occasions the time and place are filled with intercessory prayer—for the world in which the church is placed, for the church, for individuals in special and ordinary need.

Submitting ourselves to the discipline and authority of the Scriptures has kept our coming together for study and prayer from many of the perils of the cell group. It has also forged that coming together inseparably to the outward public worship of the church and, as we shall subsequently maintain, it has preserved the creative tension between our coming together and our going out to be the church in the world.

During the past two Lenten seasons the pattern of sermon seminar has been elaborated for the special emphasis of the penitential season. Our people have met in sixteen neighborhood groups or in single family groups, responding to the protest of families that the church is always pulling them away from home and from each other.[13] The exegesis has been done by radio,

[13] There is much justification for the complaint of active parish families that the church is forever urging them to be responsible parents, and at the same time calling them away from home. We are seeking to ease this real problem in our parish by having all church boards and committees meet on the same night each month, by encouraging couples to accept team assignments as church-school teachers, and by having church affairs in which the whole family may participate. The problem is far from solved, but the charge that the church is divisive is much overdone. Sometimes it is wished that the critics would make up their minds: one day the church is too "clubby," and the next day it is "divisive." Both criticisms need to be heard in the context of the church's mission, which encourages a sort of clubbiness on the one hand and a radical divisiveness on the other.

and the number of persons participating has been increased as we have sought to capitalize on the willingness of people to make some special "religious" effort before Easter. This use of radio time is an improvement over many of the devotional programs which local stations permit. For persons who cannot devote a portion of the evening to this participation in the church's preaching, there is a special repetition of the evening schedule at a seven o'clock breakfast meeting the next day.

You may be wondering what this has done to the sermon. On the superficial level it has given the minister someone besides himself to blame when the sermon lies down and dies shortly after the text has been read. On a bit deeper level it has frequently, indeed almost invariably, led the preacher where he had no suspicion he might go. This is, of course, true of all expository preaching, but it is especially true when the congregation is gathered to respond to the scripture. The preacher is not left high and dry, hunting for illustrations and relevancies. For example, the given text one week was the story of Balaam. After the sermon was prepared and delivered, I went through it and marked what had come directly through the people at the sermon seminar. Whether or not it was the Word of God I do not know, but most of the sermon in its basic orientation was "the mind of the community-before-God." [14] The suggestion of the people that Balaam seemed preoccupied with transportation led to a discussion in the group and an exposition in the sermon of means versus

[14] H. Richard Niebuhr, *op. cit.*, p. 87.

ends. Their observation that the angel of the Lord appeared where he was not expected, and that the Lord finally spoke through a faithful servant who began to balk, became part of the sermon. Later that week, as often happens, a member of the sermon seminar called with an urgent reaction. He suggested that it had occurred to him that the speaking ass might be the underdog in society, the minority, the oppressed, God's will rising up in the historical process, through the rebellion of the "imposed-upon." He related all this to arguments being presented in those weeks before our city council in regard to racial discrimination in private housing.

Even sermon mechanics sometimes come through the seminar. One man's recollection of a long and painful excursion into the Grand Canyon on a jackass could have been used, I presume, as a point of transition— the most difficult place to keep either a sermon or an ass in motion!

Occasionally a regular participant in the sermon seminar cannot be present, but registers his response to the scripture anyway. The announced lesson one week was the parable of the chief seats (Luke 14:7-11). During that week the following letter was received:

As is true most of the time, I am intrigued by the passage chosen for next Sunday's sermon. Since I am not going to be there on Wednesday evening I am writing some of my reactions. First, I am somewhat startled by the ego appeal in the parable. Don't put yourself up there because how ashamed you would be to be sent down; and do sit at the foot of the table because how proud you would be to be invited up.

And so I imagine all are going to the king's feast. (I am assuming we will all be invited—but will we?) and all gathered around the foot of the table—each of us somewhat surprised at being invited—and secretly hoping we will be moved up—maybe even way up. We are wondering why, O why is Mrs. A here and why isn't Mr. B here, etc., etc., etc. And then when Mr. or Mrs. C or Miss ———— is invited to the very head of the table—we are completely surprised. We were a little surprised that that person had been invited at all, but it is unbelievable that he or she should be so honored. Maybe some of us are really pleased. At the moment I am genuinely content to be left at the foot of the table—but would I really be? Would I think I should at least be about the middle?

As the feast progressed the king's warm hospitality makes us forget about status.

And now you will probably take off on a surprising tack and I will wonder why I was so blind.

I do not remember what surprising tack the sermon took, but I do know that some inflection of Divine Word breaks through in this person's suggestion about what happens to status before the "king's warm hospitality." The preacher dares not ignore the response of the congregation to the lesson, anymore than he dares to ignore his own.

When Richard Niebuhr wrote of the pastoral director, he also wrote in the same section of the same chapter that "the result of two centuries of Biblical criticism . . . has been an increase of the sense of the communal character of the book. For this and other reasons the best Biblical preaching going on in the churches today undertakes to interpret the Word of God as a word spoken to Israel and the Church. The minister who is obedient to Scriptures and represents its authority does so as one who is interpreting the mind of the community-before-God." [15] The interpretation of that mind is greatly facilitated by conferring with it and submitting that mutual conversation to the discipline of the Scriptures.

IV

G. Ernest Wright, in his exciting book, *God Who Acts,* defends in the preface the title he selected. It was chosen, he explains, "to point up the contrast with the more customary expression, 'God Who Speaks.' . . . The Word is certainly present in the Scripture, but it is rarely, if ever, dissociated from the Act; instead it is the accompaniment of the Act. To speak of the Bible solely as the Word, as has been done so frequently, incurs the risk of obscuring this fact with the result that the Word becomes substantive, dissociated from history and dealt with as an abstraction." So it is with the community of the church which comes together to read, hear, and interpret the Word of God. If the action of

[15] *Op. cit.,* p. 87.

the church ends there, it either has not heard the Word or has been disobedient to it. It is the hearing of the Word that both enables and directs its going out. It comes together in order to go out and be the church in the world. So Professor Wright, moving from the preface to his final chapter, writes: "But the focus of attention is not upon the Word of God in and for itself so that it can be frozen, so to speak, within a system of dogmatic propositions. The Word leads us, not *away from* history, but *to* history and to responsible participation *within* history." [16]

So the church comes together in order to go out to responsible participation within history. The world demands this of the church but does not really expect it, and there is the tragedy of the faithlessness of countless parochial churches and the strongest argument for the abandonment of the old forms altogether. The world's expectations of the church are indicated in our community and perhaps in yours by the fact that the column in the local newspaper entitled "News of the Churches" appears not on Monday, after the church has met, but on Saturday. The sad reversal; so the news is that the church *is* to assemble, not that it *has* assembled. Of course, much of the news that the church should make is not the sort that could interest the newspapers, for headlines carry less and less of news so profound is the harlotry of mass communication; yet much of the news that the church fails to make, it fails to make because it does not disperse as the church, out in the world.

[16] (London: SCM Press, 1952), p. 107.

"We are often more careful about a permanent deposit of formal truth," P. T. Forsyth told British clergymen in 1917, "than about an inexhaustible source of moral power." The situation has worsened since then with the years in between, when the church did not even check on that deposit for fear it might curb its institutional prosperity. If this be true, is it still needful to argue the merit of submitting the life of the church again to the discipline of the Scriptures, or have we found some new infallibility in councils or inner light or even the two-thirds majority vote of all members eighteen years of age or older?

Before we turn, as we do in the next chapter, to the reinvigoration of the church's "going out," the balancing response in this essential parochial rhythm, we must note that both the church's coming together and its going out are caught up and tied together in the one central act of the church, the public worship of God. If this rhythm is a dialectic, here is the synthesis: public worship. Yet that is no true act of the church at all, or at best only a distorted fragment of what that act once was and could be again, if it is a casual coming together to ask a few personal favors of some remote, mysterious, and largely benevolent god, and to sit awhile and listen to a concert of some very excellent or some very wretched music, and to hear a public address often of a general religious flavor, and then engage on the way home in a general critique of the whole performance as one might discuss the opera or the current offering at the movie house. There is no ultimate seriousness in such an exercise. With that experience behind him and before him and all about him, no wonder the layman looks at us with bewilderment when we speak of the "one central act of the church"; no wonder he can view it as incidental, not only to his vocation and his politics and his economics, but to that compartment of his life which he quietly and often reverently labels "religious."

In 1907 the Beecher Lecturer began his lectures with this sentence: "It is, perhaps, an overbold beginning, but I will venture to say that with its preaching Christianity stands or falls." [17] To be sure; but if the sermon be only a religious address, even one which has a few lines of scripture as a motto or even a whole block of scripture as an outline, Christianity cannot stand or fall on that. If preaching be only the words of one man, however devout and loyal and brave, Christianity cannot stand or fall on that, for even the best man is finite and corrupt. If preaching be only the imperative mood, the command and the commandment, the mighty "ought" of life, God's rules, Christianity cannot stand or fall on that. If preaching be just this, and if it stands at the center of public worship, then in its public worship the church will find neither the nurture promised in its coming together nor the enlargement and redirection it needs for its going out.

Yet if preaching be the corporate act of the whole church, unfolding the words of the Scriptures so that the Word in Scripture is reenacted and prolonged into our

[17] P. T. Forsyth, *Positive Preaching and the Modern Mind* (London: Hodder and Stoughton, [1907]), p. 3.

history, so the church assembled participates again in Christ, and his coming again is held in remembrance, then it is not sacrilege to speak of "our services" and to count on immeasurable benefits streaming from them to us and through us. If preaching be not simply the words of one man, but a continuation of the witness of the whole church, in its present life and in its history, in its Scripture and its councils and its hymns and its prayers, to the revealed glory and presence of God in Christ, then this one act ties together in one single harmony our coming together and our going out. If preaching is no longer the command, the imperative of the law, but the declaration, the indicative of the gospel, yea more—its re-creation; if it is no longer the words of the "ought" of life but the Word of the promise of life; then with one great Doxology, culminating in the action of the breaking of the bread and the pouring of the cup, the action which takes over when the awareness of the graciousness of God exceeds the tongue's capacity to express—then preaching, explicit and implicit, creates our coming together into worship and transforms all our going out into a perpetual act of adoration. This is to claim that preaching is not a religious talk but the primary and central human instrument which God employs for his Divine invasion of our corporate existence.

This is to claim that nowhere is the church—and hence the world in which the church is placed—so imperiled as by the fearful failure to open its whole life, its intellectual, theological life, and its corporate life of service and worship, with faithful expectation of the

descent and invasion of the Holy Spirit. So Charles Gore
wrote: "The Holy Spirit comes not so much to supply
the absence of Christ as to accomplish His presence in
the world as its Saviour and New Life." [18] Preaching, on
which Christianity may stand or fall, will arise from resources far deeper than any man's wisdom or piety, and
will move into the church to reform and to renew with
a power far greater than the words framed or spoken by
any man or school of men. To preach Christ is to re-
establish in the midst of every generation not only the
sight of the Cross but its regenerative power for the new
creation. Those who protest such an elevation of the
function of preaching in the church, and would contend
for the Eucharist or the silent mystic experience, have
not, I believe, fully reckoned with the nature both of
human speech and human history or faced the impli-
cation of the word "Word" in both revelation and the
drama of redemption. God is a God of history, and history is persons in relationship; and words—these invade,
activate, bind, relationships.

So preaching that is primarily didactic or dogmatic or
apologetic and not confessional, as we shall subsequently contend, may be the center of the sickness of the contemporary church. Forsyth's bold claim that "with its
preaching Christianity stands or falls" may be true.
There is impressive evidence from the past to support
that claim, and enough present sickness for us earnestly
to consider it again. In any event, the double movement

[18] *The Holy Spirit and the Church* (London: John Murray, 1924),
p. 110.

of the church, its coming in and its going out, is fused in public worship into one dynamic harmony, even as the most ordinary believer by his coming in for renewal at public worship simultaneously, by the witness of his coming, participates in the mighty going out of the people of God. In truth, we go out to church! Is there not among us a stirring again of the relevance and beauty of the central phrases in the old prayer for the right use of affliction, "that, when we shall have served thee in our generation, we may be gathered unto our fathers, having the testimony of a good conscience; in the communion of thy Holy Church." [19]

[19] *Book of Common Worship* (Philadelphia: The Westminster Press, 1933), p. 97.

III

THE CHURCH DISPERSED

It has been proposed in the preceding chapter that the true life of the church is nowhere so imperiled as it is by its failure to open its whole life in faithful expectancy to the promised invasion by the Holy Spirit. The church, the Body of Christ, is derived ultimately from the Incarnation, from the coming forth of God himself out of his "separate heavenly shrine into the common world to 'dwell' among men, and to suffer with them and for them"; [1] but the continuing manifestation of that coming, creative of church, is the Holy

---

[1] Quick, *op. cit.*, p. 286.

Spirit, a power not imparted to men in isolation. That community which claims to be the church, the extension of the Incarnation, must present its credentials to the world in terms of its concern for the world. That is its self-authentication. If the church is the Body of Christ, vitalized by his spirit, then it is fair to test it in terms of his work. Does it leave its "separate heavenly shrine," moving into all parts of the common world, dwelling with men and suffering for them? This is the nature of the judgment which begins in the house of the Lord. This is the nature of the legitimate question both God and the world address to the church—not only the question, Are you holy? Not only, Are you catholic? But, Are you apostolic? With such holiness and catholicity as you possess, are you always and forever being sent— moving out to man and the nations of man—with the gospel of the world's redemption, agents for the world's reconciliation?

Oliver C. Quick and others rightly maintain, I believe, that the consequence of Pentecost was a reversal in the direction of the movement of holiness. Before that gift of the Spirit

it was a movement away from the common world towards the awful separateness of God. . . . This movement of holiness is typified by the fact that in the Old Testament the centre of religious interest is in journeyings towards Jerusalem . . . but after Pentecost all is changed. The earthly Jerusalem, which was before the centre of religious attraction, now becomes a centre of diffusion or a base of operations. . . . Missionary journeys into the Gentile world take the place of pilgrimages towards the holy place where God has caused his name to dwell. The representatives of the twelve holy tribes have become twelve apostles sent out with a gospel to mankind. The movement of holiness has become a movement from God through his apostolic Church out into the common world.[2]

This observation presents itself to me as indispensable background and foundation for our consideration of the dispersal of the church into all the provinces of the world. Will you consider it as essential prelude to every concern for the dispersal of the church?

We are invited to affirm our faith in the holy catholic church, and this we do with gratitude. We must not forget, however, that each one of these two concepts, holiness and catholicity, possesses within itself the potential to hide or distort the other. The holiness of the church suggests its exclusiveness; the catholicity of the church suggests its inclusiveness; and the history of the church again and again diplays the destructive forces in that tension. How can the church be both exclusive and inclusive at the same time? It is when we see that the church is not only holy and catholic but inescapably apostolic, if it be the church of Jesus Christ, that the tension becomes creative.[3] The sense of mission, the eagerness to share every good thing with everyone every-

[2] *Ibid.,* pp. 285-86.
[3] *Ibid.,* p. 311. "The Church can be in truth both holy and catholic, because it is also apostolic, sent from God into the world with the gospel of the world's redemption."

where, this apostolic impulse is the authority within the church's holiness, and at the same time the only instrument for the fulfillment of its catholicity.

It is not difficult to think of parish churches which have been so eager to maintain their holiness that they have sacrificed their catholicity. When that happens, even a pagan outsider senses something spurious in the holiness. So we have been scornful of denominations who refuse to cooperate in the conciliar movement, and have noted the strange kinship between some such American denominations and the Roman Catholic Church, the two faces of a common fundamentalism. However, any enlargement on that distortion by the sort of churchmen who write or read Beecher Lectures may be an escape from facing the opposite problem in which we are probably more intimately involved. We are more apt to be acquainted with churches who have sacrificed their holiness in order to assure the world of their catholicity. When that happens, the world senses something unworthy or impotent in the church's catholicity. This peril of sacrificing the holiness of the church at the altar of its catholicity seems to me to be one of the most lively dangers in the theologically sophisticated American churches. With the urgency of the present push toward inclusiveness, we tend to overlook the fact that there *is* a church union born of indifference and an ecumenicity uninformed by the Holy Spirit. We need to evaluate every affirmation of the church's catholicity in terms of its apostolic mission. Wherever the ecumenical movement dominates or overshadows the missionary movement, instead of seeking to be its helpful ally and servant, the church is endangered. I do not know much about the ecumenical movement at the international level, save to rejoice in the fruitfulness of its councils and the freshness of its witness and the vitality of its struggle with the real issue of ecclesiology. But I know a good deal about it at the local level, and I wonder if in those larger international circles of ecumenicity the dangers are present, if hidden, which we experience in its smaller circles. If so, then some of the direst predictions of the "holiness" wing of the church may become sober fact to injure the whole church's highest "catholicity."

We get a hint of these perils out in the provinces when we send our laymen to work in the local ecumenical movement, and they end up happily or unhappily giving hours of time doing two things: one, they enter into conversation after conversation with other good Christians, and thus do not have time for conversation with the non-Christian and his secular or pagan world; two, those conversations are largely directed to the determination of some least common denominator of faith and opinion with which presumably the church is to confront the world. But the conversations are so pleasant and the common denominators so elusive that the world is seldom confronted, or if it is, the confrontation, based on that finally cornered least common denominator, is scarcely to be distinguished from conclusions or resolutions any group of high-principled persons might reach. The inclusion of Jews and Unitarians in such councils may create a very worthy and important organization and impress the world which has strange and perversive ideas about tolerance; but it is catholicity without holiness, and such an organization would seem to be an instrument hardly suitable for the fullest discharge of the Great Commission.

Such extreme dilution of ecumenicity into a vague and general religiosity is not uncommon, but it is grossly unfair to the tremendously significant ecumenical movement to saddle it with responsibility for all the distortions of its most distant and removed cousins. Yet I wonder if incipient dangers present in a sniffle are not more clearly to be recognized in a full-blown case of pneumonia. We are told, for example, that youth are impatient with churches, and the only valid missionary approach to a large university is the ecumenical approach. And if youth were impatient with Christ, as we were in our student days (a doctrinal impediment, we thought!), would we tone him down as we are advised to tone down the church?

No doubt there are many opportunities for the ministry of the church to a large university to be opened only in the cooperative work of the denominations concerned, just as there are many opportunities for the ministry of the church in any community to be opened only by cooperative work. The imaginative and competent ministry to migrant workers in California is one example. And the dramatic increase in the number of candidates for the ministry in the United Church of Christ is impressive testimony to the vigor and health

which can come through union of smaller and diversi-
fied denominations, who do so in obedience to the
apostolic injunction. Yet my experience suggests that
all too often the ecumenical approach at the local level
to campus or community results in more and more pro-
fessionals, ordained and otherwise, holding more and
more conferences with one another and with more and
more like-minded experts often summoned from the
theological schools to decide how to incorporate the
fewer and fewer people they are thus meeting into the
Body of Christ which, because of their ecumenicity,
must have among them *no visible reality*. That will be
the neatest trick of the week—and as the number of
converts decreases we are told that we are working *in
depth*.

Although I am aware of the disgrace and hindrance
of denominational competition and the imperative for
the American church to go abroad under a united ban-
ner and of the excitement of new conversations with
and within the Roman Catholic Church, I believe we
must continually examine the ecumenical thrust of the
church in terms of the church's apostolic responsibility.
We must protest whenever ecumenicity becomes an end
in itself or sacrifices holiness in order to be inclusive or
sacrifices inclusiveness in order to be holy, forgetting
that the whole range of ecumenical interest is the servant, not the master, of the church's apostolic responsibility.

Those of us who are the most committed to the ecumenical movement must ask ourselves, among others, questions like this: When we are able to settle the question of specific distinction between Tradition spelled with a capital "T" and traditions spelled with a little "t," and have half or more of the denominations represented recently at Oberlin all united, and hold our first big general assembly or conference or synod or council in Madison Square Garden, and decide then in our first united action, as we will be compelled to do by practical necessity, how to *divide ourselves* for administrative and liturgical efficiency; then, ah, then, will the devil really tremble any more than he does now? My hopes for the vitality of the church union under the Pike-Blake proposal were refreshed upon learning that when the invitation was actually extended to The Methodist Church and the United Church of Christ, the union was proposed as one which would be not only both "catholic" and "reformed," as originally phrased, but also "evangelical." I suspect this includes apostolic, as I have used the term. If so, let us sing the Doxology; perhaps, as some of our fathers would command, using the "long meter." But is it not ominous if "evangelical" appears as an afterthought!

This then is the overriding principle, the primary and comprehensive rule and guide for the dispersal of the church. It goes out, it is sent, it is apostolic not in order to be holy, not in order to be catholic, but because it is its essence to be apostolic; that is its nature, that is what it means to be the Body of Christ, to be that community which he has called and established and continually recalls and reestablishes by his Holy Spirit. "As my Father hath sent me, even so send I you." (John 2:21.) Even the front page of the provincial church calendar acknowledges dispersal as the essence of the church by quoting widely and repeatedly the truth that "the church lives by mission as fire lives by burning." Masao Takenaka, of Doshisha University, reminded us in a recent article of the words of K. H. Ting, of Nanking Theological Seminary: "Let us not be too sure that we have any right to say that we and our church are 'too weak' to be missionary. Let us rather say that we and our church are not missionary enough to be strong." [4] Although these words were addressed to Christians in a minority situation, they apply to the churches in the American provinces as well, who are beginning to be aware of their increasing but less dramatic minority situation.

It is in the dispersal of the parish church that the minister may be most aware of his task as pastoral director, with a good deal more emphasis at times on the "directing" than on the "pastoring." Perhaps at no other point does the futility of the minister trying to act for the whole church become as clear as when he undertakes to be the church dispersed. It is only his job to help with the dispersing. Perhaps the reputedly high rate of nervous breakdown among ministers would be reduced if we ministers would be content to perform

[4] "Toward Being a Creative Minority," *World Outlook*, February, 1963, p. 12.

the more modest and possible chores assigned us in the church, and leave some room for God and the people. Toward the end of directing that dispersal faithfully, will you consider four general observations for the minister to keep in mind as he assists his parish to be apostolic?

I

First, the parish church must be dispersed with worldly wisdom and imagination. If it is, there will be realistic and specific direction to its going out. Even where the inescapable missionary nature of the church is acknowledged in the schools or in the congregations, it is too frequently in terms of what Lesslie Newbigin describes as the missionary *dimension* of the whole life of the church in contrast to the missionary *intention* of specific aspects of the life of the church.[5] This distinction suggests to me the danger of endorsing the going out of the church in a warm, genial, broad, and general fashion, without consideration of the strategy and specifics of the going out—that is, the immediate and pressing and narrowed-down missionary "intention" of the local congregation and its members as they are dispersed into the world. The missionary intention of the parish should be spelled out winningly but clearly by its responsible officers, and it will be practical and specific

[5] Newbigin, *op. cit.*, p. 21.

if it is infused with worldly wisdom and imagination.[6] This demands a sensitivity to the behavior of persons individually and collectively and sufficient political sophistication about the actual power structures in society to avoid doing the "silly, irritating, unfair, and even harmful things" about which William Lee Miller warns in his sensible article "On Meddling." [7] That article displayed both worldly wisdom and imagination about the strategy of the church in the "church and society" question. It will satisfy neither the old social action school nor the revived each-Christian-act-on-his-own school of thought. However, Miller's hope to see fewer "answers" but more wide-ranging questions, fewer distinctively religious positions but more positions taken from religious motivation, fewer crusades but more development of civic conscience and social intelligence provides at least some direction for parishes which have been exhausted or broken by the old social action energy or frozen into irrelevance and inaction by the new worldless theologies.

Another area of particular concern where worldly wisdom and imagination are required is in the persistent problem of communication. We are told that the world in which the church is dispersed does not understand the language of the church, its Bible, its doctrines, its

[6] If this final chapter errs on the side of intention rather than dimension, of the specific rather than the general, you will at least see the consistency of my concern with that which is often elevated only to be cast down with the title of "Practical Theology."

[7] *The Churches and the Public* (Santa Barbara: Center for the Study of Democratic Institutions, 1960), p. 23.

liturgies. Protestants do not even know their own saints —like the woman who asked my secretary with ill-concealed annoyance which one of the president's family was this Studdert-Kennedy I had quoted. More seriously, the world seeks "an interpreter to translate the great, difficult, strange words of the Bible into the familiar language of daily life. The performance of this task," writes Emil Brunner, ". . . is the true service of theology—to think through the message of God's work in Jesus Christ—think it through so long and so thoroughly that it can be spoken simply and intelligibly to every man in the language of his time." [8] Well, that is easier said than done. But if the minister's professional role in the community is that of theologian, then it includes this task. But the language which is understood is not always the language of words, however basically they may be translated. Words may be the beginning and they may be the ending, too; but in between the words, prompted by the words, perhaps, and followed by them, must be the church moving, acting, being, in such a manner that it cannot be misunderstood. I shall never forget Robert Luccock's sermon in the midst of which he smashed a teacup, and a worshiper responded involuntarily and audibly, "My God!" If action were clearly established in the midst of our words, we might be surprised by the reality and spontaneity of the response.

The Fine Arts Committee of our parish arranged a display of modern art in the entrance hall of our church

[8] *Our Faith* (London: SCM Press, 1936), p. 9.

at Christmastime. People had to see it to get in to the services, including a gentle church lady who came back several times hunting for the other two Wise Men in an abstract canvas of the Magi. This exhibition raised eyebrows—often the beginning of communication. The artist spoke to some whom the preacher only confused. Recently this same committee managed some fundamental communication of the gospel by the time they had convinced the deacons that the church itself was the *only* appropriate place for the post-Easter performance of Thornton Wilder's *Our Town*. This discussion followed a previous occasion when some of our people had not quite caught the profound religious significance of the animals running up and down the aisles and around the Communion table in a production of *Noah*. When a Fine Arts Festival brought forth hundreds of examples of the creative talents of our people, the word of Dorothy Sayers that we do violence to the very structure of our being when we confine ourselves and others to uncreative activities and to an uncreative outlook was heard. The biblical doctrine of creation and of the nature of man made in God's image and the gospel of finding life by losing it were communicated in new and understandable ways. "Wordly wisdom and imagination" provided props for the preacher and new avenues of movement for the Word.[9]

[9] The parish church is often vulnerable, as I have noted in Chap. II, to the charge that it is a divisive influence in family life. The Fine Arts Festival, the production of *Our Town,* and the annual Passion Play of the old Second Congregational Church in Waterbury, Con-

Or again, if the dispersal of the church is to be marked by worldly wisdom and imagination, then the thinking and planning of the local parish must look beyond next year's "program" and be informed by the best educated guesses attainable about the future of its immediate community as well as the probable direction of the world's life. The Board of Homeland Ministries of the United Church of Christ has demonstrated what such employment of wisdom and imagination can mean in the top administrative bodies of a denomination. The local parish has the same opportunity. We have appointed a "think" committee in our parish whose official name suggests that we are more certain of its number than of its function, for it is called "the Committee of Nine." They are constituted under a bylaw which reads in part:

It shall be the duty of the Committee of Nine to keep the future of the parish *imaginatively* in mind; to formulate, review, and revise a long-range master plan, constantly anticipating the changing environment and mission of the church; to consider, evaluate, and coordinate the serious proposals of every person and group concerned with the life and progress of the church; to advise the ministers and church council in major decisions affecting the future of the church.

---

necticut, are lively instances wherein the church belies the charge that it apparently believes people are only "saved" in age groups! The adult working crew and cast of *Our Town,* for example, surrounded the younger members of the production then and ever since with the "seven fathers," which sociologists claim as a primary asset of nineteenth-century community life now lost in our urban society.

For example, they have met with the director of the city planning commission and an authority on Bay Area transportation problems, trying to anticipate the community that will be ours ten and twenty and fifty years from now. The immediate environment of the church is its immediate missionary responsibility, and the political as well as the physical nature of that environment must be known. Our local council of churches performed an appropriate function as an ecumenical body in conducting a religious census in our area recently. An analysis of the census returns by Albert Rasmussen, of the Pacific School of Religion, was a direct service by the theological school to all the churches. It revealed what we have come to understand as the "religiously displaced" in our community. They are generally of two types: members of minority races who no longer feel at home in their religious traditions, and university personnel and others who, having passed through the Unitarian and humanist stages, are now worshiping at the altar of secularism. This is our immediate missionary field. It will take both wisdom and imagination to enter it with any sort of effectiveness.[10]

[10] Over 25,000 students at the University of California are a major segment of our missionary field. They are not the religiously displaced, however, in the same sense as the two groups cited above. Members of these two groups often say that when they went to college they lost their faith and have never found it. The students, however, are their offspring, and often nowadays they do not come with a formal faith to lose. They are their fathers' children, and it may be in college that they are first confronted with the claims of the gospel. Recently a brilliant student came in to discuss religion. I lent him impressive and persuasive works of contemporary theologians. When he returned

We have learned sadly that the worldly wisdom required in the dispersal of our church responsibly to the economically and socially deprived in our community will not be exercised only toward those people, but toward our own as well. Our Negro population has grown dramatically in the past ten years, and now constitutes about one fourth of our total population and about one half of our school population. The willingness with which some of our people have agreed to face our responsibility to these new neighbors is cause for alarm and for renewed mission within the parish, for that willingness has increased as the crime rate in the community centered in the Negro population has increased. The pastoral director and his helpers begin to suspect that some of our good Christian brothers are not so concerned to save persons as to save plate-glass windows and hubcaps. The criminal activity threatens property and thereby concern for the socially deprived wins support even from the peripheral members of the parish. Here we are reminded of Reuel Howe's claim that our basic misuse of God's gifts and obstruction of his purposes are demonstrated in our constant temptation "to *love things* and *use persons*" instead of using things and loving persons.[11]

Despite these potential corruptions of motive, there

---

them, he confessed he had read the Bible instead. He said it was the first time he had ever had one in his possession or read any part of it. He was an honor graduate of Protestant-inspired American public education!

[11] *Man's Need and God's Action* (New York: The Seabury Press, 1953), p. 24.

are tremendous reservoirs of goodwill and resources of energy and money in every parish church I know, waiting for *specific* opportunities to ease the pain and hardship of other human beings. When responsible committees of our parish have put realistic and specific requests to our people, the response has always been strong. The following page was included in a brief written explanation of the approved special projects of our parish and distributed at Sunday services. From that one solicitation we had enough volunteers to launch a homework clinic for junior-high-school youngsters who needed special help or who had no suitable place to study at home, plus new workers for continuing projects.

Please fill out and place on the offering plate. As an expression of commitment to God and to the outreach of his church, I wish to consider the following service:

1. Boys' Work Project Group Leader _____
2. Boys' Work Project Sponsor or Employer _____
3. Migrant Ministry Work Camp or Exchange Visits _____
4. Worker for Half-Way and/or Part-Way House _____
5. Athletic Director at Fruitvale Project _____
6. Homework Clinic Tutor _____
7. Overseas Service _____
8. Other _____

       Name _____

       Address _____

       Telephone _____

II

Note, in the second place, that the parish is dispersed both to and through its own members. Unless we accept as normative the concept of the church as a small, closely knit, and highly disciplined fellowship, the mission of the church will always be in part *to* its own people. Perhaps this observation should have come in the preceding chapter under the heading of the church assembled, except that I am thinking of that part of the church which seldom assembles. J. Archie Hargraves has described the several categories of church members recognized in parishes which he has served. These familiar categories which exist in a number of concentric circles moving out from the lively center, where the Holy Spirit is more earnestly received, are easily identified in every conventional parish church. However, neither wisdom nor imagination suggests that these "far-out" Christians should simply be invited once again to come to church. That does not seem to have much appeal; at least, it has been tried and found wanting. Someone must go to them. The church must be apostolic right in its own front yard. But who will go? Your good, earnest, honest, devoted laymen. They are willing if you ask them, but they will tell you in advance that it won't do much good. They have been before.

Perhaps the most puzzling and promising mission field in the whole world is the one occupied by present nominal church members. As the local church moves out toward them, toward their own members through their own members, they realize how thin is the line between Christian nurture and Christian mission. We have often discovered that when we have started out with the purpose of Christian nurture, we have ended up not only with Christian nurture to the inner core of the church but with exciting mission to the distressing fringe. This has proved especially true in adult education, for example through luncheon study groups for men. We meet from time to time with our laymen during their lunch hour for a four- or six-weeks' study course. The first series of weekly meetings worked on the meaning of the atonement,[12] and the group we were meeting in San Francisco met, interestingly enough, at Bernstein's Fish Grotto. Here, trying to provide Christian nurture, we have inadvertently engaged in mission; here, trying to shore up the committed layman, we have been able to reach out and unexpectedly touch some of the most removed persons who have long been in the church but not of it. Thus, as the church moves out to its own people, it at once prepares its own people for the mission which can only move through them.

Here, alas, is the weakness in the dispersal. The mission depends upon missioners who believe it is worth their time to go out. But who is going to stop the

[12] We have since learned not to start with doctrine but with experience, and then move to doctrine. However, ministers tend, I believe, to underestimate the interest of the laymen in words like "atonement" and "incarnation," which they have long heard but seldom understood.

mouths of lions and quench raging fires and face the edge of the sword in order to deliver *valentines* to the Macedonians. How lasting a motivation for mission can be created among Christians who see no more than a martyr's death in the Cross, and who have no doctrine of atonement beyond a subjective or psychologized one? To them the embarrassing claims of the faith no longer embarrass, because those claims are no longer regarded as legitimate claims. The broad-minded, antiparticularity religionists stand rather with the Hindu who "does not believe," according to Tracey K. Jones, "that the future will belong to any one religion claiming for itself the final revelation, but that the future will see the emergence of a new synthesis of the religions. . . . Behind his [the Hindu's] thinking is the conviction that there is no final way, but that all religious truth is relative and tentative." [13] All of which suggests Chesterton's grotesque definition of religious syncretism as "religion going to pot." [14]

So it is that the church is dispersed not only *to* its own members, but always *through* them. Tracey Jones, who is an experienced statesman for missions in distant lands, claims that "the crucial problem is to help the layman see that he is the key to the future effectiveness of the mission of the Church at home and abroad. Unless every Christian is alerted and trained to his missionary responsibility, the strategic opportunities in the

[13] Jones, "All Must Go; Some Are Sent," *World Outlook*, February, 1963, p. 10.
[14] Whale, *op. cit.*, p. 130.

next half century will not be met." [15] We are hearing this on every side, but what it means has to be understood and translated into *direction* by the parish minister. Many of our laymen are attempting to accept their responsibilities to be the church dispersed, but all too often the traditional coming together of the church has not prepared them for going out. The traditional sermon may have alerted them to their missionary task, but this alert has had the primary character of mission as dimension; that is, it has not made clear the intention, the specifics, and there has been precious little else in the parish church to provide training. We have the spectacle of the enemy located and the troops called to battle, but dispersed without weapons or a plan of attack. So before the church can be dispersed it must be trained, and Christian education at once becomes something with which the whole congregation, and especially the minister, must be concerned.

The best concentrated Christian education that has taken place in our parish for a long time was a "parish forum" in the midst of a very intense political campaign. It was closed to the press, and no outsider was allowed to speak. The central issue of the campaign was a local ordinance to outlaw racial discrimination in housing. This controversy descended upon our community during Lent. The parish was engaged in the study of Galatians. On the Sunday before the scheduled parish forum the sermon was to be based on Galatians 2. The

[15] Jones, *op. cit.*

text that presented itself was Gal. 2:10, "The only suggestion they made was that we should not forget the poor—and with this I was, of course, only too ready to agree" (Phillips). The sermon was summarized and concluded thus:

This brings us inescapably to the last source of discomfort and embarrassment in remembering the poor (i.e., all the marginal persons in society.) First, our motivation is called in for examination; second, our whole social structure is involved, even politics; third, the meaning of life as well as the means of life is questioned— *and now finally and worst of all, we are personally involved.* There is no Christian remembrance of the poor in which our personal involvement is unimportant. We would like to extricate ourselves from this embarrassment by writing a check or by passing a law or by sending a representative, but in this world of persons nothing replaces our personal involvement, not what we say we will do but what we *do* do.

"What do you think?" Jesus once asked. "A man had two sons; and he went to the first and said, 'Son, go and work in the vineyard today.' And he answered 'I will not,' but afterward he repented and went. And he went to the second and said the same; and he answered, 'I go, sir,' but did not go. Which of the two did the will of his father?" So! In the present discussion in church and community about discrimination in housing, personal credentials are examined— what does the record show? Everyone I have heard *says* he believes unfair discrimination should be eliminated but the proof will not be in the *saying* alone or even in the voting, but in the *doing,* the personal involvement, year in and year out, not just in the excitement of controversy and contest but intelligent concern and personal involvement for all impoverished marginal people—as a daily way of life—not for what we may win but in response to God's undiminished and patient concern for us. In truth, the embarrassing dictum stands: Go in person if you want results. We believe that is the way God saw it, too, and that is the most embarrassing claim of all. How else is concern, caring, love, really believed and taught?

In all our talk this morning about the poor and politics and agencies and personal involvement, I've been wondering about my friend over on Parker Street. He's a fine mechanic. He keeps my car going and that takes a pretty good mechanic. He is also a Christian and he doesn't mind saying so. That is his vocation, to be a Christian mechanic! His business is closed on Saturdays, but one Saturday I drove by there with a faltering engine to see if I could find him, and he was there all right. His *business* was closed but his *shop* was open and swarming with high-school boys. The driveway was full of jalopies and hot rods and good-natured confusion. Out of the noise and industry and laughter, my friend explained to me that he and another mechanic friend open up on Saturdays and let any boy who wants to come in and use their equipment, their precious tools, even, and get their help working on their cars! And as he talked, I knew that he wasn't doing this to impress me or the boys or the neighbors or to win God's approval. I had the feeling he was saying "Thank you" to the Almighty. I am sure that is the only reason in the world Paul could have given for remembering the poor! And Christ?

"Truly, I say to you, as you did it to one of the least of these my brethren, you did it to me."

The following Friday the parish forum was held. The minister acted as moderator of the forum, and opened the meeting with an outline of several basic Christian theological presuppositions which should be determinative in Christian decision-making. The following outline of these remarks was mimeographed and distributed the next Sunday morning to the congregation, many of whom were not present at the forum.

I. *Purpose of the Meeting*

To consider a specific community problem in the light of our common religious faith, as members of the Body of Christ—Seeking together the Mind of Christ in making a particular decision.

II. *Mechanics of the Meeting*

III. *Atmosphere of the Meeting*

A. Human speech is a gift to be used responsibly. Words have power to create and to destroy. Necessity of responsible dialogue and the perils of tirades and gossip.

B. Penitence. Recognizing we are finite creatures and that there is always the possibility we may err in our judgments no matter how fervently held.

C. Regard for one another. The benefit of the doubt. We say we are here to discuss how best we may love our neighbor. It will be a strange spectacle if in the process we demonstrate the inability to love one another.

D. The church is a community of forgiveness where acceptance of one another must not be on the basis of good behavior or political agreement but in response to God's loving acceptance of us.

IV. *Some principles of Christian Faith as a Framework of Discussion*

A. Persons above things: things to be used, persons to be loved, not vice versa

B. All men are sinners
   1. This is one major theological presupposition of constitutional democracy; e.g., because all men are sinners, no one man is fit to exercise absolute rule over any other man.

   2. Laws are imperfect but essential instruments to an ordered society, but in themselves they cannot provide inner strength for the social order.

   3. Our purest motives are often plagued with self-interest, easily hidden from us.

   4. There is ambiguity in all moral decisions; but the fact of ambiguity must not be used as an excuse to avoid painful decision.

C. Emerson's dictum: "Religion is believing in what the centuries say against the hours." Necessity to maintain perspective.

113

D. Christian ethics no road to world approval or success: sacrifice, pain, cross.

E. Responsibility of Christians to be leaven in the community for justice and mercy and agents of reconciliation.

Two candidates for mayor who had taken opposite sides in the racial ordinance, both professing Christians, were asked to speak for twenty minutes on the subject of the role and responsibility of the Christian in racial discrimination in housing, and then we had over an hour for discussion. Each member of the church was allowed to question either speaker or to make a three-minute statement of his own. Even if the issues were not clarified in this one discussion, a lot of healthy emotional ventilation took place.

The proposed law had serious defects, or so some attorneys usually favorable to legislation of this kind contended, and the issues became clouded and the church and the community were sorely divided. The people discovered that they could discuss this very controversial political issue, and that the religious faith they possessed was not irrelevant to questions of property rights, the nature of law, and the pain of discrimination. Some of the irrelevancies in the discussion were tempered after one of our few Negro members spoke briefly. The meeting adjourned. There was no vote. Had there been, it would have been clear that if God's will is determined by majority vote, he holds that will most precariously at times.[16]

There were results more important, however, than resolutions by ministers—a common way for the church to pretend to face controversial issues. One result was an eighteen-inch advertisement in a local newspaper written and paid for by an individual, a member of the church, who described himself as a Republican, conservative, prejudiced, a lawyer and a doctor—for he is both—supporting the ordinance, he said, as a matter of conscience. He claimed it was the first time he had ever become involved in anything publicly. However, this one layman's witness in the community was not, to use Professor Miller's words, "a distinctively religious position" but one "taken from religious motivation";

[16] On the second Sunday after the parish forum the following statement was read by the minister from the pulpit for fear that the legitimate questions raised about this specific bill had clouded the testimony of the church in regard to racial discrimination:

"In this effort to remind you of general Christian presuppositions, I have seriously erred, if in the process I have failed to state clearly the unambiguous position of the Christian Church, as I understand it, on the fundamental issue of racial discrimination itself. Let there be no silence from either pulpit or pew on this issue, however we may differ on methods of dealing with it in ourselves and in our society. In all its social and personal forms, it is a moral disease born of hatred and selfishness and pride nauseating to the One Holy God revealed in Scripture and worshiped alike by Jew, Catholic and Protestant, a disease marked by corrosive acids which carry in them the judgment of God ultimately destroying from within unrepentant persons who foster it and bringing to ruin nations which long countenance it. Many persons on both sides of this present controversy affirm this truth. Every Christian must make his decision in the light of it. It is not a truth which we can break as we please, but one which denied will break us."

and the parish forum on the issue did not result in a "crusade," for crusades do not fare well with ambiguities and fright. However, it did help the "development of civic conscience and social intelligence."

The dispersion of the church through its people is seldom that touchy and dramatic, but it is often as difficult and divided and lacking in clarity. These missioners need training, and although we have previously suggested the peril of substituting the study group for the prayer meeting, the prayer meeting without the study group may well disperse the church only to frustration in its going out. The minister cannot expect to be wise enough or versatile enough to provide all this instruction himself, but he ought to be one who is trained to stimulate the mutual enterprise of seeking out the right questions. All the study that the church undertakes is a vain exercise if it is not undertaken with its mission clearly in mind.

The renewed and proper Protestant emphasis on Christian vocation is probably one of the chief means of the dispersal of the church. Here help and guidance from the pastoral director are welcomed and needed. He might well ask the Christian teachers and scientists in his flock to read Michael Polanyi's essay on "The Social Message of Pure Science," and come together some evening to discuss it. Is the essence of science the love of knowledge or the utility of knowledge? What will the corporation scientist make of Polanyi's claim that "in the movement which is undermining the position of pure science I see one detachment of the forces assailing our whole civilization"?[17] The pastoral director may bring the Christian politician and the Christian historian together, even if their Christianity is of the "far-out" or peripheral variety, to consider how we are to sustain the public life we treasure separated from its source. They must be asked to consider every viable answer to the problem posed by John Baillie during the Second World War and more urgent today as to how Western civilization is to survive when its purpose and ideals "are no longer allowed to breathe their native air or draw daily sustenance from their original source."[18] The asking of some of these questions may give the dispersal of the church a new thrust of power and relevance, and at the same time nurture the church and draw its periphery nearer center. Yet, these are questions that the missioners are not presuming to answer, but to ask. Perhaps the fundamental requirement of the minister in directing his people out into the world is to provoke within them the sensitivity to ask the right questions. The answers may worry us less, for God himself still has dominion over them.[19]

[17] *The Logic of Liberty* (Chicago: University of Chicago Press, 1951), pp. 3 ff.

[18] *Invitation to Pilgrimage* (New York: Charles Scribner's Sons, 1942), p. 126.

[19] We have put some of these questions in popular and pictorial form in trying to reach unchurched children. Volunteers have rung doorbells in both privileged and deprived neighborhoods revealed by a religious census to be low in percentage of families with any church connection. They have been armed with a very brief pamphlet inviting participation in our church school. Its title, "Flowers Without Roots Wither and Die," is at the top of the first page. Below is a sketch of a wither-

How easy it is, however, for a parish like ours, full of doctors and lawyers and teachers and merchants, to sense the possibility of the dispersal of the church through the vocation of its people, and how difficult that same Protestant theory must be for a parish full of people who are the vocationally trapped in our society, who belong to that increasing and futile band described by Lesslie Newbigin as "anonymous, identical replaceable units" in the social machine. Yet so long as that is true, so long as there are large or increasing numbers of persons vocationally trapped, it is absolutely inexcusable for a parish like ours not to demand that these privileged vocations be properly used as Christian vocations, as channels for the church's dispersal. Unfortunately, not all the vocationally trapped are on assembly lines. There are doctors who have lost sight of healing in the love of money; and teachers who have lost sight of students in the love of books; and ministers who have lost sight of the people in the propounding of theories. To all these people—people of our parish and people unknown—the parish is dispersed through its own people.

I have presumed to say very little specifically about the responsibility of the provincial church for what we used to call "foreign" missions, because we must encompass our own front yard and Africa's coral strands

ing plant. The drooping fruits are labeled "free inquiry," "a Bach Fugue," "free education," "public justice," etc.; the roots are labeled Moses, Jeremiah, Jesus, Augustine, Luther, etc.

in one full sweep of the Christian dispersal. I suspect, however, that one of the unresolved problems is how to engage in the "foreign" mission in such a fashion that our people really participate one by one. Indeed, this is the problem as well in any home mission beyond the immediate geographical area of the parish. Here is a place for some creative churchmanship far beyond the often artificial project plan, where a particular parish supports the left arm and half an eye of a single missionary and thus *feels* involved. We might learn something from both the Mormons and the Peace Corps, but the carping local minister should remember that no mission board yet has discouraged either funds or personnel applicants from the smallest parish. The problem of involvement of our own people is not primarily one of mechanics but of religion, and that is the pastoral director's responsibility.

III

In the third place, in directing the dispersal of the church, the minister must bear in mind God's strategy in being persistent at doors which are closed, and Paul's strategy in seeking doors that are open. We must be persistent in the mission of the church at doors closed to us, if they are crucial and important doors. Some of them are doors which we have helped to shut. One of them is higher education. My experience on the admissions committee of a university divinity school suggests that the undergraduate education of candidates for the ministry leaves something to be desired and should prompt some reevaluation of the role of the church in education, or at least encourage a renewed critique of modern education by Protestant theologians. Protestantism, which has upheld in principle and fostered free public education, may be compelled to reassess present public education and encourage the few bold public educators who still believe Cardinal Newman has not been hopelessly antiquated by the descendants of John Dewey and that truth worth considering may remain in his claim that "where revealed truth has given the aim and direction to knowledge, knowledge of all kinds will minister to revealed truth." To urge a return to the church college, and to give it new support intellectually and financially, may be one proposal to follow, but social and economic facts suggest that some new arrangements may also be required.

Perhaps the church should establish Christian residential colleges alongside the great state universities, where students using the elaborate publicly supported libraries, laboratories, and faculties can come together in living units for the disciplined study of the biblical themes, doctrines, and histories, and the works of Aquinas, Augustine, Calvin, Luther, Edwards, and others who are disastrously and insanely considered inappropriate subjects in some state-supported schools.

The exclusion of this material on the basis of an impossible absolutism in church-state relationship is a catastrophic example of the skill educated and politically free persons sometimes possess to seek to improve their countenances by hacking off their noses. There may be those who would be concerned that Christian residential colleges alongside state universities would tend to fragmentize instruction and separate students. That danger may be real, but it is scarcely as great as the danger in the assumption of most secular education that the transmission or discussion of religious tradition is either unnecessary or untouchable. Perhaps the time is here for Protestants to accept their position in a nation of religious pluralism, and understand that the minority stance carries these handicaps and demands imaginative responses, however limited they must be or however wounding to Protestant pride. Perhaps every plan for dispersion of the church must rest on that presupposition.

Although God keeps on knocking at closed doors, the Apostle sought ones that were open, and this may be part of the wisdom of the serpent Jesus commended to us. Our church in Berkeley may be alongside a great university, but it is also caught between Alcatraz and San Quentin. Parenthetically, it should be noted that since the present ministers arrived, Alcatraz has been emptied. The Scriptures have been fulfilled! Upon occasion we have heard from our pulpit a word about the contradiction between the Christian ethic of redemption and our modern penal system. Later and less dramatically and less publicly an ex-convict from San Quentin came around to give our church the opportunity to exercise a redemptive mission to ex-convicts. Now we are deeply involved in the work of the Allied Fellowship with which we did not find it crucial to agree theologically before we could move with them apostolically to those who have been in prison. For several years we have been excitingly committed to a Half-Way House in our community, where in the past year about twenty-five convicts have been reintroduced to society in the security of a Christian concern offered with the realistic knowledge that this group presented a very high risk of failure rate, for these parolees were often those who had nowhere else to go and might not yet be paroled except for this waystation. We are now considering another such Half-Way House for younger men. This small door is held open to the church by overworked and bewildered parole officers and others. It is a small door, indeed, but it is held wide open and may be one opportunity for the dispersal of the church deep into the whole problem presented to Christians by our medieval penal system.

There are closed doors at which we must knock, and open doors through which we must walk, and then there are revolving doors, never open but never shut, which if we are agile enough we may manage to get through. They ought not be overlooked. The YMCA

and the YWCA, for example, victims of a sterile ecumenism, have revolving doors as far as the church is
concerned. This would not be true, I believe, and a
reentry would not have to be negotiated, if liberal
Protestantism had been faithful in submission to the
authority of the Bible. I don't know what kind of door
is owned by the secular social agencies, perhaps one
with a glass panel. You can see in, but you can't get in.
However, you can see enough to know that insofar as
the basic problem of the impoverished marginal persons
in society is the problem of meaning, then these agencies
are officially stumped. They are stumped by their very
nonsectarian and secular nature except as they are
manned by persons who are concerned about meaning
in life as well as means; and this exception is precisely
what our Protestant forefathers presumed would be
the rule when they encouraged the government and the
schools and the universities and hospitals and social
agencies to become independent of direct and official
church control. They did not see the church as an institution among other institutions but as a people, a
people of God, a people who were dispersed into the
community to compose and frame and direct and influence its institutions. Where better for Christian vocation to be exercised, where better for the church to
be dispersed, to infiltrate, than in the humanitarian
agencies which have been pushed deeper and deeper
into the distant wastelands of secular presuppositions
about the nature of man and his Creator?

IV

Fourth and last, the dispersal of the church is of little moment; indeed, it may be only the adjournment of a club or school, if it is not confessional in disposition and method. Those who direct the dispersal of the church must reassess the role of confession in Christian apologetics. The theological revival in which we have shared, while entertaining serious questions in regard to the legitimacy of Christian apologetics, has nonetheless tended to confront the world with an apologetic in which the confessional note is conspicuous by its absence. This is not to agree with Luther, who is quoted as saying, " 'Tis a small thing that this puny breath should range itself against the sophists; what would this bat accomplish by its flapping?" [20] for that bat did flap and did accomplish much; nor is it to join the confused protest of George III, who rose up when Richard Watson published *An Apology for the Bible* in 1796 and exclaimed, "Apology for the Bible! Apology for the Bible! I did not know that the Bible required an apology." [21] Nor is this question about apologetics raised to engage in controversy over the relation between reason and revelation; but I raise it here with you at the close of this report to remind us all that, although sheer apologetics may *convince* the reason, it does not *convict* the man. The apologetics that does

[20] Alan Richardson, *Christian Apologetics* (New York: Harper & Row, 1947), p. 22 *n.*
[21] *Ibid.,* p. 23 *n.*

that is the apologetics which is also profoundly confessional. Although the point made by Gordon D. Kaufman, that a confessional position by *being* stated in any sort of intelligible terms is at once apologetic theology, it does not follow that apologetic theology is always confessional.[22] We have the strange spectacle of countless parish churches throughout the provinces served by men trained in the best theological tradition of our time, served by a people and clergy intellectually persuaded that Christ is Lord and able to argue his Lordship persuasively, but strangely inhibited from confessing him as Lord.

In October, 1740, George Whitefield came down the Connecticut Valley, preaching and exercising his phenomenal apostolic ministry. He spent only a few hours in Westfield, Springfield. East Windsor, Hartford, Wethersfield, and Middletown, but when he got to New Haven he remained three days and addressed the students on "the dreadful ill consequences of an unconverted ministry." There followed the Great Awakening of the eighteenth century. In 1960, preaching to us from East Harlem with the credentials of another apostolic ministry, George W. Webber raised the question of the scandal of the unconverted church members.[23] Certainly in this matter judgment begins as perhaps all judgment must in the house of the Lord. There is no need to belabor the dreadful ill consequences of making re-

[22] *Relativism, Knowledge and Faith* (Chicago: University of Chicago Press, 1960), pp. 10-11 *n.*
[23] *God's Colony in Man's World* (Nashville: Abingdon Press, 1960), p. 26.

ligion the servant of theology or of failing to recognize that as the church is dispersed, its power to convert is not carried in theological formulations but in confession. That confession may, in truth, be quietly enshrined in and made more persuasive by sound and systematic apologetics, but it is in no wise guaranteed by that soundness or that system.

It is embarrassingly apparent to every one of us, as he recalls his own experience in the world and in the church, that there is no argument about God's existence as persuasive as that argument which seems itself to be an actual confrontation with God because of the conviction and confession and behavior of the apologist. The saints of each generation in the parish churches and in the theological schools from whom we truly learn of Christ are not agents of God's truth to us by logic and argument, save as that logic is subject to grace and that argument is overshadowed at last by love. John W. Harvey, who translated Otto's *The Idea of the Holy,* concluded the translator's preface with this observation:

It is surely good that a book upon religion should be written by a man who feels that religion stands at the very centre and basis of life—that "the divine" in man is, in Plato's phrase, the head and the root of him—and who can make no pretense of viewing his own religion from without, as though it meant no more to him than any other. For though in so many departments in life it is the detached and unprejudiced observer who can best pronounce judgment, in this one the paradox must hold that he who professes to stand outside religion and view all the religions of the world in impartial detachment will never wholly understand any one of them.[24]

So we end where we began. It is not the sheer theological enterprise, the churchman's profession, which is creative of Christian experience, but it is Christian experience which is creative of the theological enterprise, of the churchman's profession. And the world cannot be driven to that experience by our cool, detached, rational explanation of it; but it may be drawn there by our witness to it and our constant confession of it. When that quality of witness and confession is unmistakably determinative in the theological enterprise, then it does, in fact, become creative of faith. And the theological enterprise is justified when it clears the way for that confessional note to be more clearly heard. But how will the world hear without a preacher? And the church is that preacher, the church assembled and the church dispersed; and we are the church.

> "But how are men to call upon him in whom they have not believed? And how are they to believe in him of whom they have never heard? And how are they to hear without a preacher? And how can men preach unless they are sent?"
>
> (Rom. 10:14-15, RSV.)

[24] Otto, *op. cit.*, p. 19.

PARISH BACK TALK

A Minister's Reply to the
Critics of the Local Church

BROWNE BARR

These chapters are based on the Lyman Beecher Lectures delivered by Dr. Barr at Yale Divinity School in 1963. They represent a spirited defense of the local church which, the author feels, has received too much criticism from those who have little to do with it.

Believing that new life for the church begins at the local level, Dr. Barr clearly defines the troubles besetting Protestantism in America and offers encouragement and hope for facing them within the parish church. He shows how the internal life of the congregation can be revitalized, and how this congregation can in turn make its influence felt in the community in which it lives.

To substantiate his proposals, Dr. Barr intersperses the book with examples of the ways in which a number of local churches, including his own church in the East Bay area of California, have met these criticisms and troubles and become active, witnessing congregations within themselves and their communities.